MAKERS

PARIS

MAKERS
PARIS

Kate van den Boogert with photographs by Carrie Solomon

Prestel
Munich — London — New York

© Prestel Verlag, Munich—London—New York 2020
A member of Verlagsgruppe Random House GmbH
Neumarkter Strasse 28 – 81673 Munich

In respect to links in the book, Verlagsgruppe Random House expressly notes that
no illegal content was discernible on the linked sites at the time the links were
created. The Publisher has no influence at all over the current and future design,
content, or authorship of the linked sites. For this reason Verlagsgruppe Random
House expressly disassociates itself from all content on linked sites that has been
altered since the link was created and assumes no liability for such content.

Photo Credits
p. 7 © Patti Smith (first published in the exhibition catalog *Patti Smith, Land 250*,
Fondation Cartier pour l'art contemporain, Paris, 2008); p. 48 © mk2, top left;
p. 114 © Vincent Sardon/Edouard Caupeil, top; p.184 © La Fab.;
p. 194 © Marion Berrin/Isabel Marant, left; p. 200 © Marion Berrin/Isabel Marant.

Prestel Publishing Ltd.
14-17 Wells Street
London W1T 3PD

Prestel Publishing
900 Broadway, Suite 603
New York, NY 10003

Library of Congress Cataloging-in-Publication Data

Names: Boogert, Kate van den, author. | Solomon, Carrie, author.
Title: Makers : Paris / Kate van den Boogert and Carrie Solomon.
Other titles: Makers Paris
Description: Munich ; London ; New York : Prestel, 2020.
Identifiers: LCCN 2019035364 | ISBN 9783791386225 (Hardcover)
Subjects: LCSH: Businesspeople--France--Biography. |
  Artisans--France--Paris Region--History. | Paris (France)--Description
  and travel. | Paris (France)--Guidebooks. | France--Social life and
  customs--20th century.
Classification: LCC HC272.5.A2 B66 2020 | DDC 338.092/244361--dc23
LC record available at https://lccn.loc.gov/2019035364

A CIP catalogue record for this book is available from the British Library.

Editorial direction: Holly La Due
Design and layout: Change Is Good, Paris
Production: Anjali Pala
Copyediting: John Son
Proofreading: Caitlin Leffel

Verlagsgruppe Random House FSC® N001967
Printed on the FSC®-certified paper

Printed in China

ISBN 978-3-7913-8622-5

www.prestel.com

Contents

→
Patti Smith, *Untitled (Tour Eiffel, Paris)*, undated, Polaroid,
10.7 × 8.5 cm, collection of the Fondation Cartier pour
l'art contemporain, Paris

Tower
I know everyone takes pictures of The Eiffel Tower.
But I wished to as well. It is always, to me, fresh and beautiful.
I like to look at it and imagine all the artists and poets watching
it being created. The shock of love they felt for it.
I went to photograph it in bad weather so there would
be few people; I was lucky that day, for there was no one
in sight. Only the tower and me.
  Patti Smith

Makers. They're the creative people, the ideas people, the artists, the dreamers, and all those punks with the imagination, energy, ambition, and intuition to make something out of nothing. They bring a city to life. Because, after all, what are cities but human ecosystems—networks of people breathing life into buildings and monuments, gardens and streets?

This book takes you inside the most exciting human network of Paris: its makers. It maps a section of Paris's creative DNA, detailing a piece of this dynamic human chain. Each maker introduces the next, making visible a circle of friends, collaborators, and neighbors. Meet them, then go backstage, inside their studios, workshops, and kitchens, to witness their creative processes and working lives.

The best part is, it's no secret society. These people are the engines of some of the city's most thrilling boutiques, restaurants, and galleries. Places you can visit. Entry is free! Walk through their doors to encounter a real piece of Paris, something true and rooted here and only here. Urban *terroir* if you like. Not cynical imitations nor the result of calculated career moves, not Instagram opportunities nor concepts invented by algorithm; these are fully incarnated places that are extensions of people's passions and personalities. You'll meet cooks, bakers, booksellers, cheesemakers, chocolatiers, architects, fashion designers, shoemakers, entrepreneurs, gallerists, and more. Each as singular and special as the stuff they make.

All of the makers featured here have a creative journey as unique as a fingerprint, a manifestation of selfhood. Many are autodidacts, or have invented their own professions. There is no school for what they do. They have followed their own path, carved out their own destiny, or abandoned themselves to it. And each of their creative adventures unfolds against the splendid panorama of Paris. That myth! That monument! That dream!

But this city is more than just pretty décor. Imagine it like an invisible atmosphere—a gas—intoxicating everyone in its range. In Paris, we inhale centuries of radical change, of creativity and counterculture, protest and reinvention. We breathe in the Enlightenment, revolutions, the Declaration of the Rights of Man and of the Citizen, May '68, jazz, Modernism, Montparnasse, Montmartre, and Saint-Germain-des-Prés.

Paris has always reserved a special place for its makers, and each one in this chain channels the eternal, endlessly renewing spirit of Paris, connecting every one of us to its perpetual anthem of *liberté*!

Introducing the Makers

Tatiana & Katia Levha →
Delphine Zampetti

"Delphine is a great cook, driven by passion, conviction. Before we opened Le Servan, when it was under renovations, we went to Chezaline almost every day. It's a great address, you feast on simple things that you don't find much else-where. We love the Prince de Paris ham, goat cheese and pesto sandwich, and the Spanish tortilla too. All three of us have a family life that we want to protect and Delphine has managed that very well." (p. 23)

Delphine Zampetti → Franck Audoux

"I've known Franck for quite a while now. We both used to pick up extra shifts at Café Burq back in the day, when he was working at Michel Rein Gallery and I was assistant to the artist Dominique Gonzalez-Foerster. When I go to Cravan it's a bit like going on vacation (it's our little joke). I cross Paris from my home in the 20th arrondissement and I discover another Paris: the Eiffel Tower as beauti-ful as ever, the 16th arrondissement with its architect-designed buildings, and finally his cocktails served in such well-chosen glasses. It's a real trip!" (p. 29)

Franck Audoux → Yvon Lambert

"What hasn't yet been said about the importance of Yvon Lambert on the contemporary art scene in Paris? The gallery was comple-mented for so long by the great bookshop, where he champions the book as an object of experi-mentation. A favorite medium for artists, the artist's book—which Yvon Lambert distributes but also publishes—was dear to the avant-garde between the two world wars. My book on cocktails, *French Moderne*, was imagined as a snap-shot of this era when a profusion of avant-gardes across the fine arts, literature, and music, drew society into a creative frenzy." (p. 35)

Vincent Sardon →
Sophie & Dominique Sennelier

"Sometimes I go to the Sennelier store, as much for the walk along the riverfront as because I have something to look for there. I am a very bad customer—I always leave empty-handed. The paper of too good quality, the sketchbooks bound with too much care, the colors in too luxurious boxes tend to intimidate me. I browse the shelves, everything's beautiful, everything smells good, there is the murmur of cars on the street and the view of the Louvre. It soothes me at first, and then it ends up making me anxious. I return to work at my place with my usual draw-ing tools, a marker and shitty printer paper, which I can use without feeling like I'm wrecking something." (p. 115)

Majid Mohammad → Sigolène Prébois & Catherine Lévy

"With their vases, Tsé & Tsé pay real attention to flow-ers, even if their approach is probably more Ikebana than baroque. I know that their first creation, the April Vase, was launched by the Parisian florist Christian Tortu. For him, as for me, the vase has always played an essential role in the ensemble of a composition. Personally, I rarely buy new vases, I prefer to hunt for vintage pieces." (p. 99)

Sigolène Prébois & Catherine Lévy → Vincent Sardon

"We've bought a lot of things from him, like the stamp 'Made from the remains of orphans who died of sorrow.' He has a directness that we don't have. But he's also a poet. We share his love for that simple little thing, the stamp. In our early days, when we visited workshops, we were fascinated as much by what was made as by the environment, generally old and dusty. And the panels covered with stamps—one for each function—are part of that." (p. 107)

Sophie & Dominique Sennelier →
Vincent Farrelly & Jean-Baptiste Martin

"Picasso didn't only buy his oil pastels here, but his sketchbooks too. At Sennelier we've been a reference when it comes to paper since forever. Upstairs at the Quai Voltaire boutique is our papers of the world depart-ment, where we sell all kinds of paper hand-made from banana fiber, papyrus, hemp, cotton, etc. We also sell the wonderful draw-ing and watercolor papers from the French paper mill Le Moulin du Verger, who I know also manufacture the authentic laid paper that Vincent and Jean-Baptiste use for their domino papers." (p. 121)

Vincent Farrelly &
Jean-Baptiste Martin →
Mathias Kiss

"Like us, Mathias Kiss has his creative roots in eigh-teenth-century French decorative arts. Of course, we are fans of his domino paper project decorated with a marble trompe l'oeil." (p. 127)

Mathias Kiss → Pierre Hardy

"For years now I have been creating the scenography for the shoe collections that Pierre Hardy designs for Hermès. What connects us is a contradiction: he's very masculine, very architec-tural, but he designs women's shoes; I only make angles, but this results in something delicate. There's a symmetry between us, but in different fields." (p. 133)

Yvon Lambert → Marin Karmitz

"Marin is tremendously interested in contemporary art and his collection reflects this love. When I had the gallery, he came regularly to see the exhibitions. We had very friendly relations around Christian Boltanski. He is very interested in the work of Christian Boltanski, and I am too. We had this intense topic to discuss. Even if I see him less today, it is always a shared pleasure when we meet." (p. 43)

Youssouf Fofana → Sébastien Kopp & François-Ghislain Morillion

"I bought my first pair of Veja when I was at university, a pair of volleys, I even bought two pairs, I remember. The brand had just launched and I was really impressed by what they were aiming for through their project. Veja inspired me because they are part of the first models of social enterprises that I saw in France. There was a lot going on in the ecological, ethical niche, but they were rarely wearable pieces, whereas Veja was very cool, with an environmental and social impact as a bonus. That's what I liked, and looking back, it's one of the things that inspired me a lot. We share common values." (p. 65)

James Heeley → Majid Mohammad

"I was brought up in the countryside and went to boarding school in a wild and beautiful part of the north of England close to the Lake District, the country of Wordsworth. Although I lived in London as a student, I was struck by the mineral beauty of Paris in which Christian Tortu's flower shop was like a botanical haven. His window displays were more like vitrines from a natural history museum or contemporary art gallery. It was here in his 'green temple' that my eyes opened to the world of scent. I've always seen flower shops as kind of sanctuaries in the heart of the city and I've often thought of recreating their distinctive cool and green, watery scent." (p. 93)

Benoît Astier de Villatte & Ivan Pericoli → James Heeley

"James creates perfumes that we like very much; they are very clear and precise, with very descriptive names, which correspond to his somewhat scientific mind. He is a true Parisian, elegant and nonchalant, while being a total British dandy; it's quite paradoxical. He is discreet, but also has a lot of character. What connects us is his independence; like us he refuses everything that is not equal to his ambitions, to his idea of beauty." (p. 87)

Pierre Hardy → Alain Ducasse

"Before the taste, there is the desire, if not the craving, for chocolate. Before the chocolate, there is the shop: dimly lit, the smell of the cocoa beans; to open the door is already to taste. Then, before the chocolate there is the wrapping: the kraft paper, that raw and natural protector, the names, the words, the countries. And finally, the pleasure: the melting texture, the crunch, the sweet mixed with the fruity, sharp or bitter. Alain Ducasse chocolate carefully contrives its arrival, but delivers even more than it promises." (p. 141)

Marin Karmitz → India Mahdavi

"My son Nathanaël worked with India on the Club Paradisio project, a private mk2 projection room located under the Germain restaurant in Paris. It's a little paradise of a movie theater, all curves and peacock-blue leather with a jungle décor inspired by Henri Rousseau. I also like the freshness of her hotel Le Cloître in Arles, where I often go for the wonderful photo festival The Rencontres d'Arles. I even presented my photo collection there in 2010." (p. 49)

India Mahdavi → Youssouf Fofana

"I met Youssouf Fofana because we both did a capsule collection for Monoprix. Maison Château Rouge did theirs right after mine, and I absolutely love what they did. I bought the whole collection, plates and everything, which I use all the time. It's such a happy splash of their African culture mixed in with everyday life. I think we share a certain idea of happiness and color. And they represent what's possible cross-culturally. They kept their culture but they brought it to another level and mixed it with a sort of urbanity that belongs to Paris. I think it's great." (p. 57)

Sébastien Kopp & François-Ghislain Morillion → Isaac Reina

"We love the aesthetics of Isaac Reina, the geometry and perfectly proportioned cuts. All the brand's bags and accessories are handmade in France, using French leather. Perfect for our shop, Centre Commercial." (p. 71)

Isaac Reina → Benoît Astier de Villatte & Ivan Pericoli

"What impresses me the most is that they have their workshop inside Paris. This is very rare. They manufacture almost on an industrial scale, but within Paris itself. It's pretty utopian, right?" (p. 79)

Alain Ducasse →
Apollonia Poilâne

"Our work is similar in the sense that we start with a raw material and we bring just enough technique to it to create an exceptional product." (p. 147)

Apollonia Poilâne → Jeanne Signoles

"With her leather goods company L/Uniform, Jeanne creates something between a necessity—a bag—and a luxury, just like we do at Poilâne. She adds extra poetry to the way she goes about her craft, whether by giving a number to the bags, or finding another approach to make them a little more fun. Jeanne and I met around our 'bread envelope' project. The idea was to create a bag made out of cotton and linen that would keep the Poilâne *miche* from drying out. It fits an entire loaf, and when you get down to the half loaf, you just wrap the bag around it twice. But because I work at the bakery I never need to take a whole loaf home, so when I'm traveling I use my envelope for documents, or to protect my clothes." (p. 155)

Yasmine Eslami →
Marie Macon & Anne-Laure Lesquoy

"Girl power! I met Macon & Lesquoy at a dinner hosted by Wise Women, an association of 'women of culture and creation.' I really like what they do because I value craftsmanship and manual work a great deal, especially embroidery. And they treat it in a very original, joyful, and pop way using color and ideas. For my first collection I made panties in cotton voile embroidered with delicate flowers like handkerchiefs in white, blue, and pink." (p. 213)

André Saraiva →
Yasmine Eslami

"At one point, all the girls I had love affairs with wore her lingerie, which made me want to meet Yasmine. I discovered that she was as delicious and adorable as her underwear and we became friends. We share an aesthetic style that favors simplicity, and I find her color palette quite inspired." (p. 209)

Sylvia Whitman → Isabel Marant

"I love the Frenchness of her clothes, the elegance and simplicity. I do occasionally walk down to the Saint-Germain boutique and have a browse. I have a pale pink linen shirt of hers that I love and that I've worn for years, also an electric-blue summer dress with some classic IM embroidery around the edge that is always heaven to wear. And some simple dark-green earrings that hang just right. They're clothes that are often easy to work in, climbing up ladders and reaching high for books! You'll always find a Marant fan on the bookshop team." (p. 193)

Isabel Marant → André Saraiva

"I'm pretty good friends with André Saraiva; we started out together. We're from the same generation and a bit from the same group of, how should I say, partygoers. We have known each other for a very long time. When we were around eighteen or twenty years old, we had the same gang of friends, we hung out in the same places. And it's true that I've wandered many cities in the world, and I often happen upon his little character Mr. A. It's sort of like André's stamp that tells me, 'Ah, André's been here too.' It's something quite playful and friendly that I like." (p. 201)

Marie Macon & Anne-Laure Lesquoy →
Maxime Brenon & Julien Crespel

"We often go on our creative voyages with Julien [Julien and Marie are a couple]. We take advantage of these trips to visualize common inspirations that will be treated completely differently by the two brands. We also use these trips to pool our commercial contacts and introduce each other to buyers we know. And lastly, we share information about manufacturers in terms of their quality and reliability. We are pooling our resources more and more. As we are small companies, there is often no point in integrating certain skills in a permanent way, so we work with freelancers who spend a few days each month in each of our businesses. Other companies in our network like Kerzon use the same service. This allows the freelancer to work full-time between several entities and we avoid having to work with large structures, which are too expensive for us." (p. 221)

Christophe Vasseur → Pierre Coulon

"One can practically survive on bread and water. Then you add a piece of cheese, and it's the Cretan diet! Like me, Pierre is an anti-industrial activist who champions and perpetuates artisanal and farm traditions. His cheese manufactory, like my bakery, is a small urban factory where we produce food artisanally in the heart of the city, using quality raw materials. And dairy products are very important for us too; after flour, butter is the raw material we use the most." (p. 235)

Maxime Brenon & Julien Crespel → Christophe Vasseur

"Julien lives across the road from Du Pain et des Idées, so as soon as there is an event in the office, big or small, we pick up the best *viennoiseries* in all Paris there. There's always a reason to pop in! Of course, we are mad about the praline rolls and the *niflettes*, which we scarf down in about two seconds." (p. 229)

Jeanne Signoles →
Victoire de Taillac-Touhami &
Ramdane Touhami

"I met Ramdane when I was studying econo-metrics in Toulouse in the mid-1990s. We are of the same generation and used to hang out in the same places. He has always been at ease with anyone, and we have in common an open and curious mind. Today, we are neighbors in Saint-Germain-des-Prés. We opened our shop a little over a year after Buly inaugurated their beautiful rue Bonaparte space, and Ramdane and Victoire were among our first customers. Moreover, it is thanks to Ramdane that we found the site on Quai Malaquais; he was very attentive to our project and typically enthusiastic. I am also a client of L'Officine Buly: the Eau Triple with orange blossom or honey are my favorites. And I always have one of their scented candles on my desk, like the Alexandrie scented with mint, lemon, and black currant." (p. 161)

Victoire de Taillac-Touhami
& Ramdane Touhami →
Marie & Alexandre
Thumerelle

"We started out together. We were in the same group of friends. When I opened the Épicerie with Artus de Lavilléon in 1998, there was a small Ofr. corner. We did things together that worked, and things that didn't work. Now Alex is our neighbor in the Marais, a very local guy, a hippy in sandals! And like us at Buly, Ofr. is a family business." (p. 169)

Marie & Alexandre Thumerelle →
Agnès b.

"We've met her a few times. She intro-duced me to Jonas Mekas at the Centre National de la Photographie for exam-ple. We drank vodka together, it was joyful. When I was making movies, I was very flat-tered that despite my young age she agreed to lend me clothes for the shoots, like a first reader who validates the seriousness of my scenario. I remember articles in the news-papers where she cited us as an example, 'the place that inspires me today ...' for our improvised, jazz side and the day-to-day-ness of it; the idea of the 'shop-house.' She continues to inspire me. I know that she is still 100 percent responsible for her business, that she always has the final say on everything. She continues to open many people's minds, it's magnificent! She has a point of view. She has really participated in Paris, with her places, her spirit, and all the stuff she has bought from artists—her collection is huge! Thank you for them. Alongside the prevailing cynicism, she continues to live with her heart." (p. 177)

Agnès b. → Sylvia Whitman

"I have always had a special relationship with books. My first husband Christian Bourgois was a publisher, it's the b. of my name. I really like Shakespeare and Company. It is a beautiful and inspiring bookstore with such a special atmosphere. There are so many stories, but for me it's a place that is forever tied to the history of the Beats. I knew the poet Gregory Corso, he was a great person, and a very loyal friend. I made him a beautiful poet costume in brown velvet. I was touched when Sylvia gave me a first edition of one of his collections of poems. I have a lot of ties in this neighborhood, there are many beautiful things there: the secondhand booksell-ers, many antiques dealers, then rue Gît-le-Cœur not far away." (p. 185)

Pierre Coulon → Jacques Genin

"The trouble I have with certain pâtissiers is that they use glucose instead of sugar—dehydrated fruit, vegetable gums, colorings, and all that crap. What I like is simplicity, making very good things with little. I could send a whole team over to Jacques Genin for his lime and basil tart." (p. 241)

Jacques Genin → Yves Camdeborde

"I've known Yves since the 1990s. He's served my caramels and choc-olates in his restaurants since the days of the Régalade. I love his cook-ing, it's as generous as he is. Lies are not possible with him, he always stays true to himself. And he's some-one of great generosity. Whenever things have been difficult, Yves was the person who came to see me every day. He is profoundly humane." (p. 249)

Yves Camdeborde →
Tatiana & Katia Levha

"I saw them start out in the busi-ness. I sensed the same convic-tion, the same passion that I had when I started in 1990. They resemble me, but they're not copying. It's important to under-stand the past, but to live in one's own time and generation. Like me, Tatiana learned the trade working for the big names, and made the decision to express her personality, her roots, her way of seeing things. Family is vital too. Increasingly I think cooking is becoming homogenized interna-tionally; Tatiana champions cuisine with personality." (p. 15)

TATIANA & KATIA LEVHA

Chef, restaurateur
Le Servan, Double Dragon

Raw cuttlefish, green papaya, sesame-Sichuan cream, minced pork; calf brain, lemon butter sauce, sorrel; crispy pork belly, green vegetables, clams, ginger; asparagus, smoked mayonnaise, tofu, katsuo. This series of mouthwatering haiku is taken from the menu of the Levha sisters' award-winning Parisian bistro Le Servan. Drawing on both a multicultural heritage and a mastery of French culinary technique and traditions, chef Tatiana spices up local produce with an abundance of fresh herbs, chili, lemon, and exotic condiments for an inspired fusion cooking style.

After abandoning studies in literature and languages, Tatiana entered Paris's prestigious Ferrandi cooking school in 2005. Here she met her partner, the precocious Parisian chef Bertrand Grébaut of Septime fame, who has been by turns an essential model, rival, and champion throughout her career. After Ferrandi, Tatiana gained experience working alongside two of France's most influential and inspired chefs. At Astrance, Pascal Barbot is famous for incorporating exotic influences into a contemporary French style. And is there anything left to say about the legendary Arpège, where Alain Passard transforms biodynamic vegetables from his own garden into edible koans?

Meanwhile, Tatiana's younger sister Katia was getting training and experience in the hospitality industry, studying at a hotel school in Switzerland, then working in restaurants in Paris and a palace hotel in London while developing a passion for natural wines along the way.

Tatiana was just twenty-nine years old and Katia twenty-five when the pair opened Le Servan in 2014. The relaxed but stylish bistro was immediately filled with happy diners—and critics! French food guide *Le Fooding* awarded it Best Bistro for 2015. In 2018, the Levha sisters followed up the success of Le Servan with Double Dragon, a no-reservations spot that serves a more spontaneous rendition of their cultural heritage and childhood spent between the Philippines, Hong Kong, Thailand, and France.

With their restaurants, the Levha sisters are at the heart of a new generation of young chefs and restaurateurs that define Paris's contemporary dining scene today. A scene where French tradition and terroir are dusted off to become the raw materials for personal expression, creativity, conviviality, and fun.

→ At Le Servan, your bill comes in one of these battered old tins Katia likes to pick up at flea markets.

Tatiana & Katia Levha

Why do you do what you do?

K: Running a restaurant together is something we've wanted to do since we were very young. When you really want something, there's a sense of urgency. And it didn't feel too difficult, even if it's been lots of work, but we've been very lucky with many things. It took off immediately.

A life-changing meeting?

T: Evidently, Bertrand Grébaut is important in both my working and private life. He's been very important in the work choices I've made, in the desire to start my own restaurant quite quickly. Because he opened his quite soon after finishing school. He started two years before me and on the whole he has stayed two years ahead. We are good work companions.

What's a typical day for you?

K: We get here at 9 a.m. We place the orders with the suppliers. These conversations to find out what's good, what's new, are a daily routine. Everyone is very passionate, so they're enjoyable exchanges. We inspect the deliveries, we check that everything's there, that there are no problems. Then we prepare lunch. At 11:15 we eat together, at 11:40 we return to work. The service starts at noon, until 2:30, 3 p.m. After, we get back to it at 5, 5:30 p.m. for the dinner service. We try to see and talk to each other as much as possible because that's what makes everything work. Since we opened Double Dragon, we see each other less and we miss not working together as much.

↑
Le Servan and Double Dragon are very much a family affair. The sisters both have partners and young children and have carefully organized their working life to accommodate both. Le Servan is closed on weekends and Monday lunch (as is Septime, the restaurant of Tatiana's partner chef Bertrand Grébaut), meaning they can spend time together on the weekends.

How do you explain your success?

K: In all modesty, Tatiana's cooking. For me, it's the best, and it's something we believe in. We also have great suppliers with whom we've been working from the beginning and who provide us with wonderful materials to work with. They are beautiful things to share.

What inspires you?

T: Rather than inspiration, I work according to constraints. Constraints really drive creation in fact: the kitchen, the team, their size, the workload, the customer, the season, the price of ingredients, the quantities available. What is possible or not with what we have. It's the unifying theme, and it's restrictive in a good way, it prevents us getting distracted. We have the chance of having access to everything in Paris, so it's good to have some constraints that help us focus and produce something coherent.

What is your favorite neighborhood in Paris?

T: The 11th arrondissement. It's a very mixed neighborhood, there are people from everywhere. And at the same time there is a real dynamic around food, in a broad sense—restaurants and shops—there's a real local clientele for that. So you eat well, and it's a nice family neighborhood to live in with your kids.

↓
French Bordier butter lined up next to fermented black bean sauce and Japanese Tosa vinegar, a fermented black rice vinegar flavored with bonito.

Le Servan

ZAKOUSKIS

BULOTS, MAYONNAISE AU PIMENT 10€
COQUES PIMENT BASILIC THAÏ 10€
RADIS, BEURRE D'HERBES 8€
WONTON DE BOUDIN NOIR, SWEET CHILI 10€

ENTRÉES

RAVIOLIS DE JOUE DE BŒUF, CHAMPIGNONS NOIRS, JUS AU VIN ROUGE, MOËLLE 16€
VENTRECHE DE THON ROUGE CRUE, BRIOCHE TOASTEE, PIQUILLOS ET PIMENT FRIT 19€
MOUSSERONS DE LA SAINT-GEORGES, ARTICHAUTS, AIL NOIR, MOZARELLA GRILLÉE 19€
SEICHE CRUE, PAPAYE VERTE, CRÈME SÉSAME-SÉCHUAN, PORC HACHÉ 15€
ASPERGES BLANCHES, VINAIGRETTE CRÉMEUSE AU VIN JAUNE, POUTARGUE, NAVETS NOIRS 16€
CERVELLE DE VEAU, VINAIGRETTE CRÉMEUSE AU VIN JAUNE, BEURRE CITRONNÉ, OSEILLE 13€

PLATS

THON ROUGE DE LIGNE MI-CUIT, CAROTTES AU BBQ, SAUCE VIERGE À L'ORANGE SANGUINE 29€
POITRINE DE COCHON CROUSTILLANTE, LÉGUMES VERTS, PALOURDE, GINGEMBRE 26€
CANARD DE CHALLANS, POMMES DE TERRE, NAVETS GLACÉS, XO 27€
RIS DE VEAU, ÉPINARDS, GRIBICHE À L'HABANERO 40€

FROMAGE ET DESSERTS

SELLE-SUR-CHER ET NEUFCHÂTEL DE LA MAISON QUATREHOMME, SALADE 12€

FEUILLETÉ AUX POMMES, CARAMEL, GLACE VANILLE 9€
TARTELETTE FRAISE-RHUBARBE, SORBET FROMAGE BLANC 9€

↑
Le Servan's short menu is reconfigured daily, depending on mood,
season, and provisions.

→
Le Servan prepares their own pickled
chilies and flavored vinegars, this one
is infused with garlic and tarragon.

Le Servan, Double Dragon

↓
Spring onions are a staple in Chinese and other Asian cuisines; chervil is one of the four traditional *fines herbes*, along with tarragon, chives, and parsley, essential to French cooking; and dill is the emblematic Mitteleuropean herb, used to flavor everything from borscht to Polish pickles. With a French-Polish father and a Filipino mother, Tatiana's multicultural heritage is often memorably translated into a dish.

Tatiana & Katia Levha

VISIT

Le Servan
32 rue Saint-Maur, 75011 Paris
Roquette, METRO: Rue Saint-Maur or Voltaire
www.leservan.com

Double Dragon
52 rue Saint-Maur, 75011 Paris
Saint-Ambroise, METRO: Rue Saint-Maur
Instagram: @doubledragon_paris

NOSE TO TAIL

Start your meal at Le Servan with a glass of wine and a couple of *zakouskis*, the Polish word for appetizers made for sharing. The black pudding wontons with sweet chili sauce have been a fixture on the menu since the restaurant opened. Typical of Tatiana's cooking style, this dish combines French and Asian flavors. As well as black pudding, you might also find calf brains, sweetbreads, tongue, beef cheek, or duck hearts on the menu, as Tatiana follows a sustainable "nose-to-tail" ethos; "if you're going to kill the animal, it seems only polite to use the whole thing," to quote pioneering London restaurateur Fergus Henderson.

Tatiana & Katia Levha —

DELPHINE ZAMPETTI

Cook
Chezaline

Delphine Zampetti owns and runs Chezaline, a perfect, modern little deli in the 11th arrondissement. By noon every day there's a queue running out the door. A self-taught cook, Delphine grew up in Bordeaux where she went to art school before moving to Paris to work a variety of jobs, including set design for film. She remembers feeling dejected by the meals delivered on set. "One day it's Italian, the next Vietnamese, or Japanese, and in the end everything tastes the same; it was hard on long days to not eat well." After having her son Diego in 2005 with her partner, Chef Iñaki Aizpitarte of the restaurant Le Chateaubriand, she started working part time with a photo studio, catering shoots, which is how her career as a cook began. After a few gigs in the kitchen at some cool foodie spots in Paris (notably the gourmet wine bar with attitude, Le Verre Volé) she decided she wanted to open her own place, as working nights on top of parenting had become too exhausting.

Chezaline is a revamp of the classic French *traiteur*, a sort of deli where dishes—typically French or regional classics—are prepared for takeout. But at Chezaline these fusty old recipes are given a makeover, precisely cooked and seasoned, then served cold in delicious gourmet sandwiches. Crunchy baguette or a soft sesame bun are filled, depending on the day and the season, with chicken pot-au-feu, herring, rabbit, smoked haddock, or Spanish tortilla. Delphine also likes to prepare beef tongue or cheek. "Offal is great for Chezaline because it can be stewed in a sauce and kept warm." And there are always a few veggie options too. Then the fillings are expertly garnished with perhaps fresh herbs, mayonnaise, pesto, tapenade, or pickles.

← If Delphine had a lot of experience cooking before setting up Chezaline, the direct contact with the clients was new. "We can't hide; we're not in a hidden kitchen." She enjoys the feedback and interaction. Here her assistant Raphaëlle makes final adjustments to the counter before the lunch rush.

Each day Delphine adjusts the menu depending on what she's prepared for the day. A hot dish of the day is also available—today beef cheek stew served with celeriac and parsley tabbouleh—and the leftovers will be recycled the next day as one of the cold fillings for the sandwiches. "Alain Ducasse came by just after we opened and he chose the rabbit sandwich, which reassured me that I could actually reuse hot dishes from the day before by transforming them into a cold filling. I was really happy that he chose that sandwich."

→
A classic French entrée, eggs mimosa, are on the menu at Chezaline every day: remove the yolks from hardboiled eggs and garnish with a dollop of homemade mustard mayonnaise, then grate the yolks over the eggs, sprinkle with chopped chervil, and serve.

←
A vintage sign asks clients to check their change at the till. "No complaints will be accepted afterwards."

Delphine Zampetti

↑
Above the knives hanging on the magnetic strip, stacks of retro bakelite plates and plastic baskets in pastel hues conjure an old-fashioned canteen vibe.

Why do you work where you do?

I fell in love with this place, this old butcher shop from the 1950s with its yellow tiles and Formica and the horse head out-front. It suits my personality. I wanted to open my own place but I only wanted to open during the day. When I came across this place with its big cold room and refrigerated display, I said to myself, "That's it, I'm going to open a deli!"

What inspires you?

I felt that there was a lot of trauma originating in the school canteens in France, where everything is overcooked. So I wanted to make those recipes, but make them appetizing.

What's a typical day for you?

It's very intense, even if it's great to be finished at 4 or 4:30 p.m. We arrive at 8:30 a.m., the fresh produce is delivered and we begin to prepare the recipes for salads or sandwiches. We have two hot plates and an oven, so it requires some gymnastics to be organized. We go and get the bread. Usually I keep the dish of the day warm in the oven. During service I put the stews and other slow-cooking recipes on and leave them to cook for 2-3 hours, ready for the next day. If we've put something precious on like rice pudding, we need to be careful not to forget it!

Your greatest influences?

We cooked a lot at home when I was little. And then my partner Iñaki Aizpitarte is a chef; I saw his evolution and liked it. I wanted to do it too.

What do you consider your greatest achievement?

I am very happy that I love my place, and that I have my clients, some of whom I see every day. I think this is the most important thing, to have regulars. It's what motivates me. When I prepare a salad or a sandwich I say to myself, "If he comes in today he'll be happy."

↑
The sandwiches at Chezaline are made with a choice of a soft round bun or half a baguette. "I looked around and tested all the bakeries. And finally I talked with Maison Landemaine over the road and they make the *baguette tradition* how I want it. It's a good size when it's cut in two and cooked golden how I like it. If it's overcooked it hurts the palate, but if it's undercooked there's no crunch."

↑
Delphine's bestseller is the chicken pot au feu: whole chicken cooked in broth with carrots and a bouquet garni, then cooled, deboned, and mixed with a mustard vinaigrette, gherkins, shallots, celery, and dill. "It's very tasty. I can't take it off the menu! I like slow-cooked dishes. They're different when eaten cold."

→
The *jambon-beurre* is the classic French sandwich, available in just about every bakery in the country. Delphine's version is prepared to order with good salted butter and freshly sliced ham. And not just any ham. The ham "Prince de Paris" is prepared by a local company with a traditional recipe and without preservatives, giving it exceptional flavor and texture.

Delphine Zampetti

BEHIND THE NAME

Delphine opened her deli inside a former horse meat butcher shop, or boucherie chevaline as it is known in French. She kept the original façade with the golden horse head outlined in neon above the door, and just replaced the "v" of chevaline with a neon "Z", and voilà her place had a name! Horse meat is falling out of favor today in France, but it was popular, particularly with working-class France, throughout much of the twentieth century. It was declared legal for human consumption in 1866, just before the outbreak of the Franco-Prussian war, but food shortages experienced during the French Revolution and the Napoleonic Wars had led the poor and the starving soldiers to eat horse meat before then. And legend has it that the French classic steak tartare was inspired by the fierce horse-riding tribes of the Mongolian steppes, the Tatars, who would tenderize slabs of horsemeat under their saddles all day and then eat them raw for dinner!

Chezaline
85 rue de la Roquette,
75011 Paris
Roquette,
METRO: Voltaire

Delphine Zampetti —

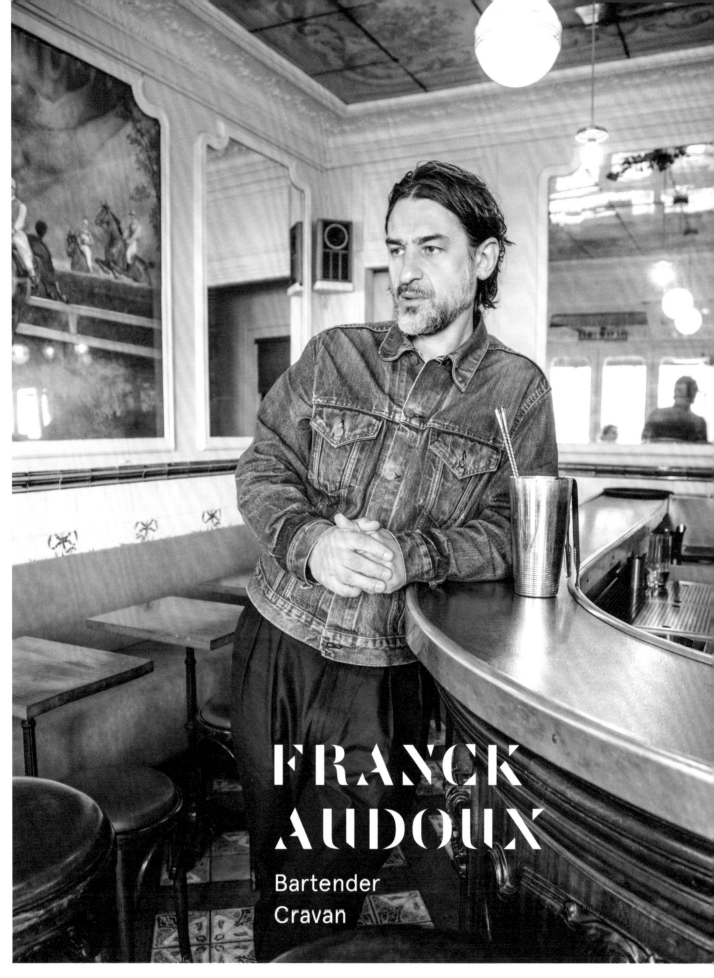

FRANCK AUDOUX

Bartender
Cravan

Like a concept album, every element in Franck Audoux's radical cocktail bar and café—its name, its original Art Nouveau interiors designed by Hector Guimard, the Tannoy speakers streaming jazz, the vintage Baccarat crystal tumblers—anomalously contributes to a complex narrative whole.

Franck opened Cravan in 2018, the same year he published *French Moderne*, a book of cocktail recipes that offers "a kind of cultural snapshot of an era, and shows how the cocktail, like jazz or the Charleston, participated in the reconstruction of a new society after the carnage of the First World War." Cravan's identity is similarly rooted in the hedonistic and groundbreaking decade or two that came after 1918, the dawn of the modern age, when Paris was a buzzing cultural capital in which cocktails had a role to play.

Cravan stands as a synthesis of Franck's eclectic background. While studying history in his native city of Tours, Franck started working for local contemporary art gallery Michel Rein. In 2000 he followed the gallery to its new location in Paris, then a few years later he cofounded the pioneering restaurant Le Chateaubriand with three friends, one of whom is the rakish, self-taught chef Iñaki Aizpitarte. With a free-spirited cooking style, focus on natural wines, and punk attitude, Le Chateaubriand delivered an uppercut to the Parisian dining scene when it opened in 2006, influencing a whole generation of bistros since. In 2011 the group opened Le Dauphin next door, a natural wine bar set inside a cool Carrara marble box designed by Rem Koolhaas and Clement Blanchet, serving creative small plates from the same kitchen.

Cravan has some things in common with Le Chateaubriand: a décor left practically as they found it; a bold, unexpected location in an overlooked neighborhood; and an obsession with achieving perfect flavor balance. Cravan is a rare exercise in focus, simplicity, restraint, and quality, orchestrated across a note-perfect menu of cocktails, coffee, and bar food (no beer or wine), stripped of nonessentials like ostentation, ego, and fancy garnishes! What you will find is a very modern dedication to pleasure in the avant-garde spirit of 1920s Montparnasse.

↗

"When you start getting interested in cocktails, you always end up collecting books." Belonging to Franck's personal collection and dating from 1929, *Cocktails de Paris* is a legendary collection of recipes. Compiled by Rip, aka Georges Gabriel Thenon, a Parisian dandy, entertainer, and writer of popular revues of the time, and illustrated by his friend Paul Colin, a famous set and costume designer and one of France's great poster artists, many of the recipes originate from cocktail-making championships of the day.

→

A dish of white asparagus and tuna bresaola pairs well with the acidity of the Yellow cocktail: gin, gentiane, and yellow Chartreuse. Open from early in the morning to late at night seven days a week, Cravan serves breakfast items like eggs, granola, and porridge, then continues with a sophisticated and seasonal all-day bar menu with offerings like lobster roll or Onsen tamago. On Saturdays and Sundays, the weekend roast is prepared with exceptional Allaiton lamb and paired with the perfect Bloody Mary.

Each cocktail at Cravan is served in a glass that has been carefully selected to complement the drink, a mix of premium new pieces and vintage ware. Seen here are gold-rimmed "Nick & Nora" glasses and coupe glasses from New York City's Cocktail Kingdom, vintage Baccarat crystal pieces, and tumblers from the UK's Urban Bar.

→
The original Café Antoine, which Franck rechristened after the poet, critic, and prankster Arthur Cravan. "An American couple came here, and the woman introduced herself as Arthur Cravan's granddaughter. Her mother was the daughter Arthur Cravan had with Mina Loy. She showed me photos of her grandmother taken by Man Ray, some Duchamps they have at the house...."

Franck Audoux

31

If the cocktail is an import from the US, France can lay claim to the aperitif. And Franck is a master of French heritage spirits such as Cointreau, Byrrh, Bénédictine, Chartreuse, French vermouth, Suze, and Pernod that he often incorporates into his cocktails. Generally infused with plant or herb extracts, these aperitifs are often highly aromatic or bitter and stimulate the palate prior to dining. "The cocktails we offer at Cravan are more pre-dinner cocktails that favor aromatics over strength."

What is your motto?
"Art is what makes life more interesting than art."–Robert Filliou

Who is your hero?
Arthur Cravan, of course. Oscar Wilde's nephew, a poet and boxer who landed in Paris in 1910 and founded the literary review *Maintenant*. A colorful character, he stole Duchamp's mistress, the artist and writer Mina Loy, then apparently drowned in the Gulf of Mexico around 1918.

Describe your profession.
The search for a kind of perfection, for maximum effect through minimal implementation.

Your favorite tools?
The eye and the palate.

What is your favorite neighborhood in Paris?
The bridges of Paris where you can see the horizon, both horizons! To cross the Seine is to remember why you love Paris and why you live there.

What is luxury?
Freedom ... and a good tailor.

↑
An original fresco decorating one of the walls of the café. At the turn of the century, the early cocktail bars in Paris—known as American or New York bars—were men-only bars where racing was a fervent topic. Paris's Longchamp Racecourse can be found not far from Cravan, inside the nearby Bois de Boulogne.

←
One of Franck's current favorites, a highly aromatic version of the classic champagne cocktail in which a sugar cube infused with Angostura bitters is dropped into a dose of cognac then topped up with champagne. Instead, Franck uses reductions of champagne and Angostura bitters to concentrate their flavors and bring out the tannins in the champagne.

VISIT

Cravan
17 rue Jean de la Fontaine, 75016 Paris
La Muette, METRO: Jasmin
Instagram: @cravanparis

ARCHITECTURE

Cravan is located within a historic ensemble of seven Art Nouveau buildings designed by the architect Hector Guimard. Taking up an entire block, 17 rue Jean de la Fontaine is a protected historical monument whose facade is as original and iconic as the café's interior. But Guimard's most famous legacy is surely the entrances he designed for Paris Metro between 1900 and 1913, many of which remain in place today (many were also demolished). Much criticized at the time for being too extravagant, the sinuous structures in cast-iron and glass were inspired by organic forms like insects and plants. More buildings designed by Guimard can be found at 14 and 60 rue Jean de la Fontaine. At the turn of the century, this wealthy, residential neighborhood was a laboratory for Modernist architecture; a short walk away you'll find early experiments in reinforced concrete by Le Corbusier and an entire street of masterpieces by Robert Mallet-Stevens.

Franck Audoux —

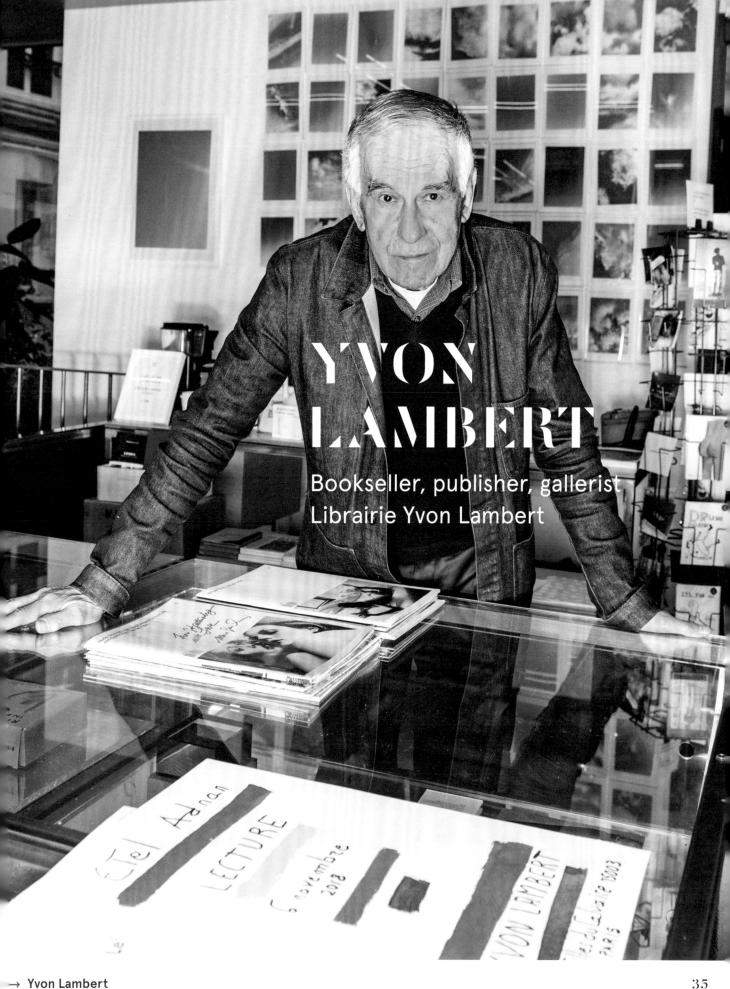

YVON LAMBERT

Bookseller, publisher, gallerist
Librairie Yvon Lambert

In 1964 the young American artist Robert Rauschenberg took home the top prize at the Venice Biennale, sending shockwaves through the art world. An American artist winning the Golden Lion for the first time heralded the decline of Paris's domination over the international art market, the rise of the New York scene, and Pop as a major new contemporary art movement.

Yvon Lambert felt the vibrations. In 1964 he was twenty-eight years old and for a few years had been running a small gallery in his hometown of Vence near Nice, on the French Riviera, where he showed drawings by Modigliani or Picasso, who lived nearby. Even with the region's dense population of artists, Yvon wanted to come to Paris. "I didn't want to run a nice little gallery in the south of France." But he wasn't interested in promoting the academic art of the School of Paris either; he was more attuned to the new forms of expression his own generation was exploring: Pop art, Minimalism, Conceptual art, Land art.... In 1965 he opened his gallery on the Left Bank and by 1968 was defending a whole new generation of largely American artists that he had discovered on trips to New York and introduced to Paris, including Carl Andre, Lawrence Weiner, Robert Ryman, Brice Marden, and Cy Twombly.

For over forty-five years until he closed the gallery in 2014, Yvon Lambert was a cornerstone of the Paris art scene, committed to discovering and championing "the best of what's new." In 2002 he opened a bookshop adjacent to his gallery, now located in the Marais, asserting his commitment to books and publishing, a passion he had been pursuing in parallel to his work as a dealer and gallerist.

Today, in a beautiful space designed by the architect Dominique Perrault, the bookshop presents a dense and beguiling selection of art books, magazines, catalogs, artists' books, rare and out-of-print books, limited-edition prints, posters, DVDs, T-shirts, and an array of art objects—all informed by a lifetime of engagement with art and ideas. And a small "white cube" at the back of the shop allows Yves to continue to articulate creative encounters and passions via exhibitions.

→
A bookshelf in Yvon Lambert's private office. "That's really me, all that stuff. That's my corner."

↑
Yvon Lambert's desk. Not just art, literature too.
In 2019, Éditions Yvon Lambert published the first
French translation of the novel *Llefre de tu* by experi-
mental Catalan writer Biel Mesquida, with a preface by
Mathias Énard and a cover specially illustrated by the
Spanish painter Miquel Barceló.

← Many limited-edition posters for past exhibitions are for sale in the bookshop. Here a poster by Cy Twombly for the 1972 exhibition *Actualité d'un Bilan*, a retrospective Yvon presented of his young Parisian gallery at the invitation of the trailblazing Festival d'Automne of Paris. In Twombly's signature scrawl, the poster lists the participating artists like Carl Andre, Marcel Broodthaers, Daniel Buren, Christo, Sol LeWitt, and Lawrence Weiner, a generation linked to Conceptualism, Minimalism, and Land art.

↑ The bookstore looks and feels a lot like a gallery. On the wall by the entrance hangs a selection of works for sale—prints, drawings, photographs, posters—by artists associated with the gallery, including Basquiat, Quentin de Briey, Jamie Hawkesworth, David Shrigley, and Cy Twombly.

Yvon Lambert has always published exhibition catalogs to go along with his exhibitions. In the 1970s he started publishing more critical works. Here are a few books from the bilingual collection *Mot pour Mot / Word for Word*, including the first in the series published in 1979, "The Daily Images of Power; On Kawara from Day to Day," a portrait by the philosopher René Denizot of one of the founders of Conceptual art.

→

Running the length of the bookshop, a wall of birch plywood shelves is an integral part of Dominique Perrault's architectural project. The books are arranged face-out, flat, or stacked in horizontal or vertical piles. Mini vitrines are installed within the shelves, allowing for thematic edits of books and objects.

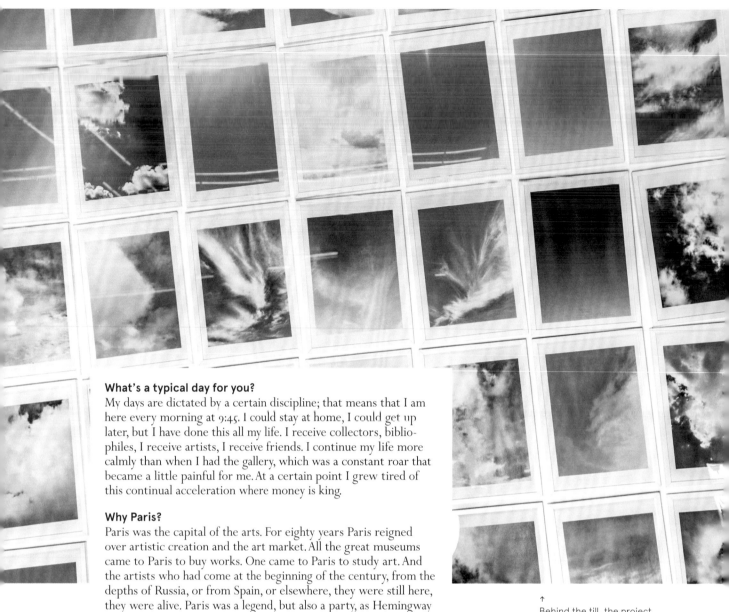

What's a typical day for you?

My days are dictated by a certain discipline; that means that I am here every morning at 9:45. I could stay at home, I could get up later, but I have done this all my life. I receive collectors, bibliophiles, I receive artists, I receive friends. I continue my life more calmly than when I had the gallery, which was a constant roar that became a little painful for me. At a certain point I grew tired of this continual acceleration where money is king.

Why Paris?

Paris was the capital of the arts. For eighty years Paris reigned over artistic creation and the art market. All the great museums came to Paris to buy works. One came to Paris to study art. And the artists who had come at the beginning of the century, from the depths of Russia, or from Spain, or elsewhere, they were still here, they were alive. Paris was a legend, but also a party, as Hemingway said. It was where things were happening.

Your greatest influences?

It has been a tradition since the end of the nineteenth century to ask artists to work on books. Ambroise Vollard, who was a very important dealer, made a magnificent book called *Parallèlement* with Pierre Bonnard and Paul Verlaine in 1900 after Verlaine was dead. And Kahnweiler made magnificent books with Picasso. I feel like an heir to the people that made these books—they are role models for me.

How do you explain your success?

I loved this work so much, I loved these artists so much, that nothing, nobody could prevent that. There is faith too; to believe in it. I decided to keep that faith.

Describe your profession.

My profession is an eternal new beginning. To live with the adventure of creation is the beauty of my job.

↑
Behind the till, the project "Yesterday" by David Horvitz. Every day the artist emails a photo of the sky to the bookstore indicating the date, time, and location the photograph was taken. It is printed out on A4 paper with an office printer and sold online and in the shop for 1 euro for one day only. Since Horvitz lives in Los Angeles, the photographs arrive the next day in Paris. The bookstore collaborates regularly with Horvitz and has even installed a micro-gallery curated by him, the Matsutake Gallery, inside a cupboard at the back of the shop.

↑
Yvon Lambert publishes artists'
books, or *bibliophilie*. His collection *Pli selon Pli* presents a work of
art folded within a hard cover and
published in a limited edition of
just fifty copies. A kind of portable
artwork, it can be stood on a table
or windowsill or mantelpiece. Here,
the first in the collection, by Etel
Adnan, from 2017, "Nuit."

→
Stacks of framed pictures in the
corridor of the bookshop. On the
far right, "Fragments," a photograph
by François Halard, shows a detail
from inside Yvon's villa in Avignon in
the south of France. He purchased
the house a few years before donat-
ing over 550 works, about a third of
his personal collection, to France.
In 2000, the Collection Lambert,
a unique contemporary art museum,
was inaugurated inside the magnificent eighteenth-century mansion
the Hôtel de Caumont in Avignon.

Librairie Yvon Lambert
14 rue des Filles du Calvaire,
75003 Paris
Northern Marais,
METRO: Filles du Calvaire
shop.yvon-lambert.com

ARCHITECTURE

In 2017, a few years after the gallery closed, the bookshop moved to a new site in the northern Marais. Yvon immediately knew he wanted to work with his friend Dominique Perrault on the project. One of France's most important architects, Perrault was commissioned by President Mitterand to design the now emblematic National Library of France, a fine example of Minimalist architecture. And his radical redevelopment of Paris's landmark Louvre post office is set to reopen in 2020, redefining that neighborhood. "I asked Dominique to come over and we had lunch in a small bistro nearby. He saw the space. He took a paper napkin from the restaurant and immediately he drew the long shelf that runs the length of the store."

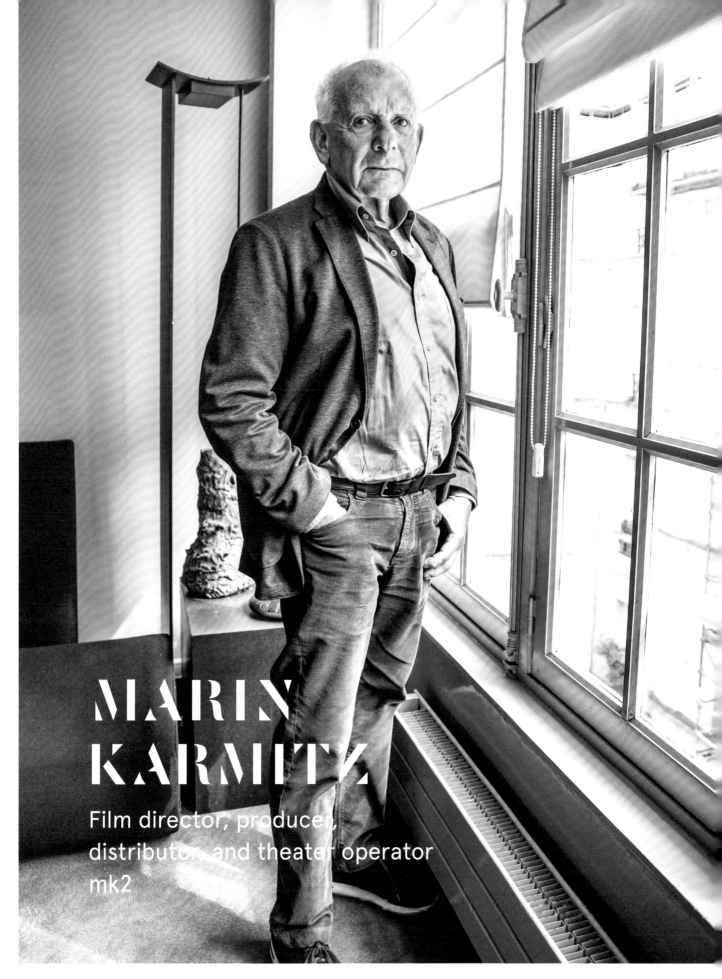

MARIN KARMITZ

Film director, producer,
distributor, and theater operator
mk2

Marin Karmitz is the founder of the French independent cinema empire mk2. Comprising production and distribution arms, but also a chain of art-house cinemas, the company has helped shape the history of cinema for half a century and counting. Since the late 1960s, mk2 has produced well over a hundred films by greats from Jean-Luc Godard to Xavier Dolan and has distribution rights to a formidable catalog of master works from the likes of Charlie Chaplin, François Truffaut, and David Lynch. Committed to showcasing unique work from around the world mk2 defends a "certain idea of cinema"—cinema that matters.

The humanist, modern culture that Marin Karmitz injected into his company was partly born out of the political and cultural upheaval of May 1968, when a Leftist student revolt on the Parisian Left Bank led to a massive general strike—the biggest in French history—that paralyzed France and almost toppled the government. Marin was one of a generation of dreamers and revolutionaries who marched the streets waving banners with slogans like "Put imagination in power!" or "Be realistic, demand the impossible!" deeply influencing France's subsequent cultural and political landscape.

Marin was 30 years old in May 1968, but his political awakening had begun as a high school student, around the time he moved to Paris from Nice with his family. The Karmitzs were a wealthy family of secular Jews who had immigrated to France from Bucharest in 1947, surviving the Nazis only to flee the communists.

After training as a cameraman at the IDHEC film school, now La Fémis, in Paris, Marin started his career working as assistant director to filmmakers of the Nouvelle Vague, the French New Wave, including Jean-Luc Godard and Agnès Varda. In 1964, he directed his first short, *Dark Night, Calcutta*, based on a screenplay by Marguerite Duras, then worked with Samuel Beckett on a film adaptation of his play *Comédie*. Marin's first feature-length film *Seven Days Somewhere Else* was released in 1967, the same year he set up his production company, mk2 Productions.

In the slipstream of May 1968, he directed two films that engaged with the critical debates of the time, *Comrades* (1970) and *Blow for Blow* (1972). Then in 1974, partly motivated by his frustration with the traditional film system's refusal to distribute his films, Marin launched a distribution company mk2 Diffusion, and opened his first movie theater too. Now with the whole circuit locked down, Marin could truly back the filmmakers he believed in and get their films made and on screens around the world. Today his sons Nathanaël and Elisha are at the helm of mk2, continuing to fight for new voices and stories to be heard.

↑
Three portraits hang above Marin's desk. In the middle, a painting of his paternal grandfather and namesake that his parents "snatched from the hands of Romanian robbers" before fleeing the country. On either side, black-and-white portraits by the French photographer Patrick Faigenbaum. On the right is a portrait of the Czech intellectual Karel Cerny, who was "first put in a concentration camp by the Germans, then by the Russians. You can see it in his hands."

→
Many souvenirs scatter Marin's office, including this photo of Marin and Juliette Binoche on the set of Krzysztof Kieślowski's *Three Colours*. Left of that is a drawing *A Dance to Karmetz* by the New York cartoonist Jules Feiffer.

↑
Among the works of art stacked against the walls, this portrait of Marin by his friend the French painter Gérard Fromanger. *Drapeau Français (Le Rouge)*, another work by Fromanger, decorates the foyer of the mk2 Bastille cinema complex today. The French flag was also the basis of *Film-Tract n° 1968* that Fromanger made with Jean-Luc Godard in 1968, a three-minute continuous shot showing the red of the French flag dripping over the other stripes. You can watch it on YouTube.

↓
A few of the more than 150 awards and nominations Marin Karmitz has received throughout his career. Mk2 productions are fixtures at film festivals in Cannes, Venice, Berlin, Hollywood, and beyond. And among the awards, memorabilia from the successful pharmaceutical business (Droguerie Standard) the Karmitzs once owned in Bucharest.

Marin Karmitz   47

MARIN KARMITZ IN 10 FILMS

Cléo from 5 to 7 (1962)—Agnès Varda

I was assistant to Agnès Varda on *Cléo from 5 to 7*. Agnès Varda was my second teacher. I was lucky because with her I began to unlearn what I had learned at film school and to reflect on modern cinema, that is, the Nouvelle Vague—new ways of producing, new ways of thinking about cinema. And this has served me all my life.

Blow for Blow (1972)—Marin Karmitz

In *Blow for Blow*, workers in a textile factory go on strike and occupy the factory. These were the sort of questions we were asking ourselves as intellectuals or artists post 1968. I feel so fortunate to have lived through that time in France. It taught me a lot, it made me think about cinema from a political perspective. But I paid very dearly for my political commitments. *Blow for Blow* was my last movie, I was boycotted afterward.

Every Man for Himself (1980)—Jean-Luc Godard

Jean-Luc made a remake of *Blow for Blow* that was a huge flop despite starring Jane Fonda and Yves Montand. It made our relationship a little difficult for a little, and no one wanted to work with Jean-Luc anymore. He went to Grenoble for a while and did great things with video. A few years later I produced *Every Man for Himself,* which was his greatest success.

Half a Life (1982)—Romain Goupil

In 1982 I had more than a dozen films in competition at Cannes and took home five awards. Romain Goupil won the Camera d'Or for best first feature with *Half a Life*. I also had the Palme d'Or for *Yol* ("*The Road*"), the Grand Prix for *The Night of the Shooting Stars* by the Taviani brothers, Best Screenplay for Skolimowski's *Moonlighting*. We also had Madonna's first film *Smithereens* by Susan Seidelman in competition that year.

Mélo (1986)—Alain Resnais

I remember Resnais was very respectful of my production imperatives and succeeded in expressing his directorial freedom within the constraints of a 21-day shoot, and a final cut that did not go over 105 minutes.... *Mélo* was a success!

↑
Posters for the last two films Marin directed: *Camarades* (1970) by Bernard Dufour and *Coup pour Coup* (*Blow for Blow*, 1972) by the satirical cartoonist Jean-Marc Reiser—films steeped in May 1968 ideology, concerned with workers' rights, capitalism, consumerism, and American imperialism. "If I was blacklisted as a director after *Blow for Blow*, May 1968 led me to think about cinema as a site for counterculture. Cinema as a de-compartmentalized, interdisciplinary space connected to literature and music, conferences, photography, and so on."

Three Colours: Blue, White, Red (1993–94)—Krzysztof Kieślowski

Three Colours, three films: Liberty, Equality, Fraternity. It was about six years of work, between the decision to make them, writing the scripts, shooting, then the release. A film is a bit like a marriage, it's something very intimate: You live with the director so you need to get along, otherwise you cohabit in extreme conditions of conflict, which is awful. So the stakes were particularly high. With Kieślowski it was pure joy, the very difficult work we did really united us. I was truly happy making these movies.

La Cérémonie (1995)—Claude Chabrol

I made twelve films with Chabrol, that's a lot. We worked together for 20 years and he had many successes. With Chabrol it was the same situation that I had with Louis Malle, Alain Resnais, and Godard, which is to say very important directors who had made flops, so no one wanted to make the films that I went on to produce.

Code Unknown (2000)—Michael Haneke

I like this film a lot. It's a great movie, it's a film about Europe, which I practically commissioned. I said, "Maybe you, as an Austrian, can make a film about Europe, because you must sense what Mitteleuropa really is." He made this film about people fallen on hard times, people unwanted by their society: African people, Romanians, gypsies, French people. Then we made a second film, *The Piano Teacher*, which won the Grand Prix at Cannes.

Paranoid Park (2007)—Gus Van Sant

Produced with my son Nathanaël, we were proud to present one of Gus Van Sant's most experimental films at Cannes in 2007, where it won the 60th Anniversary award. I first met Gus when we distributed his film *Elephant*, the second film in his "death trilogy." For me, *Paranoid Park* seems to transform this film series centered on teenage angst into a tetralogy.

Matthias & Maxime (2019)—Xavier Dolan

I was lucky enough to meet Xavier Dolan through my son. This is the tenth film we've worked on with him. There's the joy of seeing dazzling talent. There's that little flame, like in the film *Quest for Fire* (1981), you know, that flame that is protected and moved from territory to territory so that people can warm themselves, and eat. Cinema continues.

↑
A work by the German artist Dieter Appelt, *The Mark on the Mirror Made by Breathing* ("*Der fleck auf dem Spiegel, den der Atemhauch Schafft*") hangs in Marin's office. "I think the question we can ask ourselves is 'Why are we in the world?' One answer for me is the presence of the other; it's what makes us not alone, to be in otherness, in the necessity to take into account the other. And the most present, the most immediate otherness is the face and everything that it contains: looks, smiles, tears. The face and the human body have enormous importance for me, they tell me stories."

→
The maquette of the mk2 Bibliothèque cinema designed by architect Jean-Michel Wilmotte. As well as art house cinema, mk2 movie theaters are also founded upon an urban and architectural vision. "There was a hole at the foot of the National Library of France that no one knew what to do with. Nobody wanted it, and I filled the hole. You see how the neighborhood has changed. It is a really interesting urbanism project that we participated in. Because there was nothing here in the aughts, and now we have 1.8 million spectators per year; it's the third most popular cinema in France. And this at an edgy arthouse cinema screening films in undubbed versions, with a lot of very different films, a lot of events, with a bookstore.... Here again, we demonstrate that cinema can change lives."

VISIT

MK2 Bastille–Beaumarchais
4 boulevard Beaumarchais,
75011 Paris
Bastille, METRO: Bastille
www.mk2.com

CULTURAL HUB

The first cinema that Marin Karmitz opened in 1974 remains at the heart of the Bastille neighborhood's cultural life today. Marin's radical new model established art house movie theaters in overlooked, working-class neighborhoods and integrated other cultural or lifestyle elements too, like art, books, cafés, and music, turning the theaters into cultural hubs that revitalize local communities. Today mk2 operates more than ten cinema complexes in Paris. "Bastille was the first cinema I opened. It was born at the same time as the *Libération* newspaper. When I did this, undubbed cinema in Paris was only screened in the Latin Quarter, everywhere else screened dubbed versions. I am very proud to have been the first to impose subtitled, original versions of foreign films in all my theaters. We did a lot of crazy things, and it was a crazy idea. Our idea wasn't to make cinema, it was to use cinema to change the world."

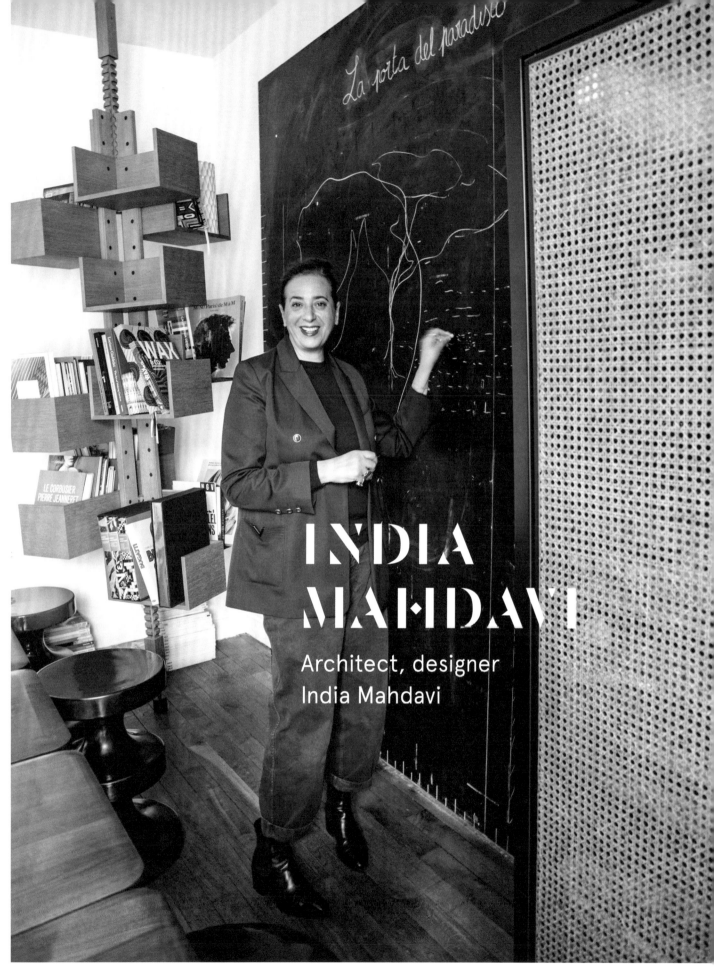

INDIA MAHDAVI

Architect, designer
India Mahdavi

India Mahdavi has been bringing her colorful and cosmopolitan sensibility to public and private spaces—hotels, restaurants,
bars, boutiques, private homes—in France and around the world
for more than two decades. Born in Tehran in 1962 to an Iranian
father and a half-Egyptian, half-English mother and named
after the country in which she was conceived, India spent a
nomadic childhood traveling around the world with her parents
and four siblings, from Iran to Cambridge, Massachusetts;
Heidelberg, Germany, to Vence in the south of France. Her
unique style marries organic forms, bold colors, and lickable
textures—a sort of synthesis of Hollywood, Bollywood, and
the French Riviera. Bubble gum, mint, teal, mauve, celadon,
egg yolk, and mandarin. India uses color as an element to inject
energy, light, and joy into all her projects.

Saturated in (techni)color and exotic atmospheres, her
projects have a real cinematic feel, and indeed India had once
dreamt of becoming a filmmaker. She enrolled in architecture
school—inspired by the architect-trained film director Fritz
Lang—at the École des Beaux-Arts in Paris to learn about space
and composition while waiting to apply for a post-graduate film
directing program. But by the time she graduated from architecture school, her focus had shifted to set design, and she left
Paris for New York, rounding out her education there with studies in industrial, graphic, and furniture design.

In 1990 India returned to Paris and began working for the
renowned interior designer Christian Liaigre. Her experience
there was a revelation in that the design process began with
a detail of a texture or a material from which an entire project
would then be expanded, rather than starting with an architectural blueprint and working down.

Following the birth of her son, India decided to go solo, opening her studio a couple of years later in 1999 on rue Las Cases,
around the corner from her home, allowing for an easy coordi-
nation between work and home life. From this base in Paris, her
projects take her around the world, an ambassador for her very
own international style.

← →
Even if there is a laptop and a monitor on her desk,
India prefers to work directly on paper. She tends
to design using a collage-like process, cutting up and
recomposing the original plan with tracing paper that she
draws on with her Pilot Sign Pen. "I cut a lot. I cut, I paste,
and I use white-out. I print out and then I cut things and
I re-tape them."

In every corner of India's office you'll find a jumble of art, ornaments, souvenirs, and curios. Here a portrait of her son Miles by his father Derek Hudson hangs on the wall. "The day I had my son changed my whole career because it made me think about what I wanted to give him, about transmission, basically. What kind of life did I want to lead? Suddenly you become an adult in the sense that you put your life in perspective." On the right, a wooden model from the cinema project Club Paradisio in Paris shows how India transformed an angular site into something soft and round. The gold statue is an award from the Salone del Mobile in Milan for "Best Designer at The Design Prize 2018." The piece of black velvet is embroidered with the word "who" in Arabic.

Below a silkscreen print by Herzog & de Meuron and Ai Weiwei illustrating their collaboration on the 2012 Serpentine Gallery Pavilion, a composition of contemporary and vintage lamps and vases on a shelf. On the far right, the Beirut Heavy Light by Lindsey Adelman next to a white vase India Mahdavi designed for historic French porcelain makers Bernardaud.

↑
Installed inside a grand former apartment, India's creative studio maintains
an inviting, homey vibe, furnished mainly with prototypes and house designs.
A double salon at the entrance connects the meeting area with a more relaxed
area with sofas. The many bookshelves are organized thematically: art, travel,
history, fashion....

→
On the left a vintage rattan piece, on the right one of a series of masks India
has developed using this material common in the 1950s and 1960s. The
cartoon theme is a nod to her years spent in the US as a child. India has also
developed a series of furniture designs—a table, bench, mirrors—using rattan,
but with a complex marquetry technique. She likes to confront this modest
material with a refined artisanal finish.

↑

"Every project is the start of a new story. It's like building a scenario. And to
convey that story you can use words, but you also want to use a few images
to help the client understand. We can find images of spaces, but also images
of movies, atmospheres … it's more about a feeling. And it's super difficult
to actually express that feeling before you start a project, but you have to
convince somebody of something: Is this the direction you would like to go?"

↑
A miniature 3-D portrait of India next to models of the Charlotte furniture she designed for Sketch's Gallery restaurant. Restaurateur Mourad Mazouz commissioned India along with British artist David Shrigley to create a new concept for the space, which has become London's "most Instagrammed restaurant." "By using pink in a very monochrome, dramatic way, and creating a very immersive situation, Sketch kind of created history. I think it inspired a lot of people to use color."

What is unique about your work?

At India Mahdavi we create, we produce, we sell, and we distribute. So it's many professions in one. One activity can feed another. This makes me very independent and autonomous. It's also a way of being very sustainable. And it's a way of defending my own vision, of being authentic. Our small scale allows me flexibility and independence too, and means I keep a direct contact with my clients. I know who they are, I know what they like. There's something real about it.

How do you explain your success?

Sometimes there's just a whole bunch of little things that add up. It's my exotic name. It's my background. It's the fact that I'm a woman. And I'm also an amalgam between the Middle East and the West. I'm a mix between different religions, different educations. I think it's actually what the world is about today, and my work is the expression of all of that.

Describe your profession.

I think there are so many similarities between how I work in my profession and the movies. You have a producer, and there's the filmmaker, and then you have the actors, who are the people who animate the spaces, and then you do promotion in the same way. The similarities are quite amusing; I'm in the entertainment business in a way. I bring joy to people by telling a story. I see it a bit like that.

What is luxury?

What is it? Is it wasting? Is it overproducing? Is it throwing away? Is it running after money? How far are we going to go? How do you consume? How do you produce? All these questions are super important to me. And I think that luxury doesn't have to be about belonging, it doesn't have to be about buying, it doesn't have to be about consuming. I think it should be about sharing. I think luxury today could be keeping your integrity. It's about being responsible because we're coming to a point where things are becoming a bit dangerous.

↑
A peek into India's personal cabinet of curiosities—a black lacquered cabinet where India stores all sorts of little treasures used to spark ideas or memories and organized by material and texture. Here there is a focus on china and ceramics, but other drawers might privilege marble, wood, or enamel.

RUE LAS CASES

Since India opened her studio in 1999 on rue Las Cases, halfway between the Eiffel Tower and Saint-Germain-des-Prés in Paris's posh 7th arrondissement, she has gradually expanded into three storefronts downstairs. Here she showcases the furniture and other objects—lamps, textiles, mirrors, etc.—that she develops for and with her clients, such as her signature ceramic Bishop stool, or the Charlotte armchair she designed for Sketch in London. Like a suite of film sets, each space has its own atmosphere and configuration. First came the elegant furniture showroom in 2003, then in 2012 a gorgeous clutter of a shop for "small objects," and then in 2019, a gallery space. "rue Las Cases is my *casa*, it's about being physically anchored in Paris. I opened my showroom when I realized that in France they thought I was based in London or New York. The world has become very local and at the same time I've managed to also become quite global. I kind of like that mix."

SOME DESIGN PROJECTS BY INDIA TO VISIT IN PARIS

Le Germain
25 rue de Buci, 75006 Paris
www.germainparis.com

Thoumieux
79 rue Saint-Dominique, 75007 Paris
www.thoumieux.com

Le Café Français
1-3 place de la Bastille, 75004 Paris
www.cafe-francais.fr

India Mahdavi
Invalides, METRO: Solferino
www.india-mahdavi.com

Showroom
3 rue Las Cases,
75007 Paris

"Petits Objets" Shop
19 rue Las Cases,
75007 Paris

Gallery
29 rue de Bellechasse,
75007 Paris

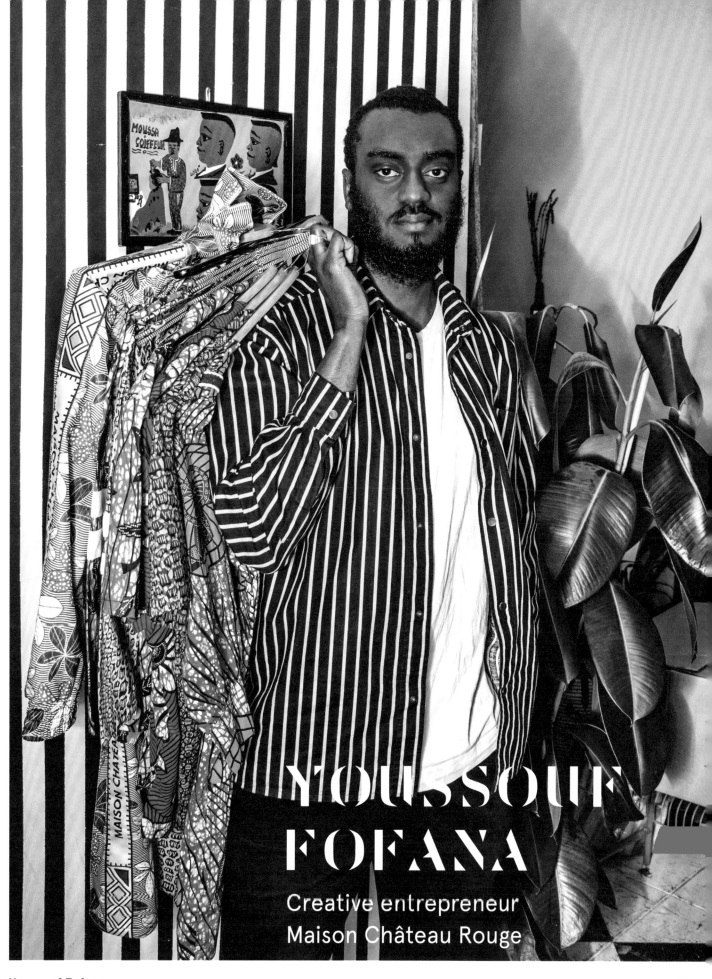

YOUSSOUF FOFANA

Creative entrepreneur
Maison Château Rouge

Youssouf Fofana is still trying to catch up with the success of his fashion label Maison Château Rouge. Channeling the spirit of Paris's "Little Africa" neighborhood in the 18th arrondissement, Maison Château Rouge met with immediate and unexpected success when Youssouf quietly launched it online in 2015. The cool street looks combined with bright African wax fabrics captured a certain zeitgeist and the pieces sold out in a flash. Soon Maison Château Rouge was picked up by Paris's most influential concept and department stores—from Merci to Le Bon Marché—with all sorts of high-profile collabs to follow. In 2017 Youssouf was even invited to join President Macron's entourage on his government's first state visit to Africa.

But initially the idea was simply to help fund other projects by selling a few T-shirts. Maison Château Rouge is an extension of the nonprofit Les Oiseaux Migrateurs ("The Migrating Birds") he set up a year earlier with his brother Mamadou as a vehicle for ambitious development projects in Africa.

One of seven children of immigrant parents from Senegal, Youssouf and his brother, like much of the African diaspora, have been sending money back to their village since they have been of working age. They set up Les Oiseaux Migrateurs with the goal of helping to build sustainable solutions that would create economic independence for these communities. Their ambitions continue to grow across both fronts—fashion and social development—as Youssouf works at building bridges between both his African and French cultures and the rest of the world with projects that are deeply personal, creative, and socially engaged. Maison Château Rouge goes from strength to strength and counts an evergrowing number of followers, collabs, and sales points internationally. The image of the *Parisienne* gets a dose of Afrocool at last.

↑
Each wax pattern has a story. Though when they leave the factory in Holland or England, they just have a reference number. It's the local traders and distributers in Africa that give them a name, with local relevance, as a marketing tool. For example, "the swallow pattern was reissued in the Ivory Coast during a civil war. As all the swallows are flying in the same direction, they called this fabric 'Reconciliation' as a sign of harmony and peace."

←
Each collection has a theme. For SS20, Youssouf was inspired by the University of Timbuktu, a collective of three mosques in Mali that have been an important intellectual center in Africa since the Middle Ages. "I thought it was important to tell this story too because the history of African cultures or African countries is not well-known—we know about slavery and colonization, and that's all."

↑
"This is the first Château Rouge piece that we made. It's a garment with a
contemporary cut but using traditional fabric. It represents me and the neighborhood too. I was born in Paris, I grew up here, but I have an African soul that
is strong because my parents come from there. And Château Rouge is a neighborhood in Paris with an African soul. A mix of cultures created this garment,
but also my personality, and this neighborhood too."

←

As well as African wax fabrics, Youssouf is inspired by folk art, particularly the sort found on the many hand-painted signs seen throughout West Africa and the Congo. Here, a few from his collection, including a hairdresser's menu displaying some of the different cuts available for men.

MAISON
CHÂTEAU
ROUGE.

↑
Youssouf gets inspiration for each new collection from
clothes he notices on the street or on Instagram.
He makes sketches and collects screenshots; when
it's time to work on the collection he pulls out everything
he's assembled over the preceding months and makes
new sketches, then decides what's relevant and coherent.
All before he starts on the fabric selection: "the fabric
is the essence and the soul of a garment."

←
Maison Château Rouge often incorporates these hope-
ful, life-affirming messages commonly found throughout
Africa—written on the side of a bus, a car, or a shopfront—
into their collections. Here, a hand-painted sign bids
"Bonne Arrivée" which translates to "welcome."

Describe your profession.
What is my profession? I don't know if I'm a creative or an entrepreneur. I was a project manager once and I think that what I mostly do is project management. Today with all the new professions and ways of working, everyone is a project manager.

What is unique about your work?
For me entrepreneurship is really important. I'm convinced that in a society like ours, entrepreneurship is a key factor that allows you to change things and to have your say. Which is especially important as children of immigrants. Our parents immigrated to France for economic reasons; part of that was to help the families who stayed behind have better lives. Today we are a new generation and we have new methods to help our families back in Africa. I think that happens through the autonomy of local populations and their entrepreneurial efforts.

How do you explain your success?
Today the world is changing with social networks, etc. For a long time, trends were dictated from above and today they come from below. It's the people who decide what is a trend or not.

Why do you work where you do?
Château Rouge is the African district of Paris. My uncle had a shop at 30 rue Myrha years ago; he was one of the first to have a shop selling wax fabrics in the neighborhood. And I often came here with my mother to buy vegetables, to buy fish, etc., but also to buy fabric. When you are of African descent in Paris you know Château Rouge. Everyone knows this neighborhood, in France but also in Africa.

Describe your atelier or office.
I'm also inspired by the style of the Memphis Group. That's why we have lots of stripes in the shop. I think there's something very African in the Memphis style; when I see drawings by Nathalie Du Pasquier, I see a lot of similarities.

What is luxury?
It amused me to call the brand Maison Château Rouge. "Maison" evokes the luxury industry, and Château Rouge we know is a working-class neighborhood. It was important for me to confront the two worlds, because for me luxury today is not necessarily about having an expensive garment, but one that is authentic and culturally rich. And we have that in this neighborhood.

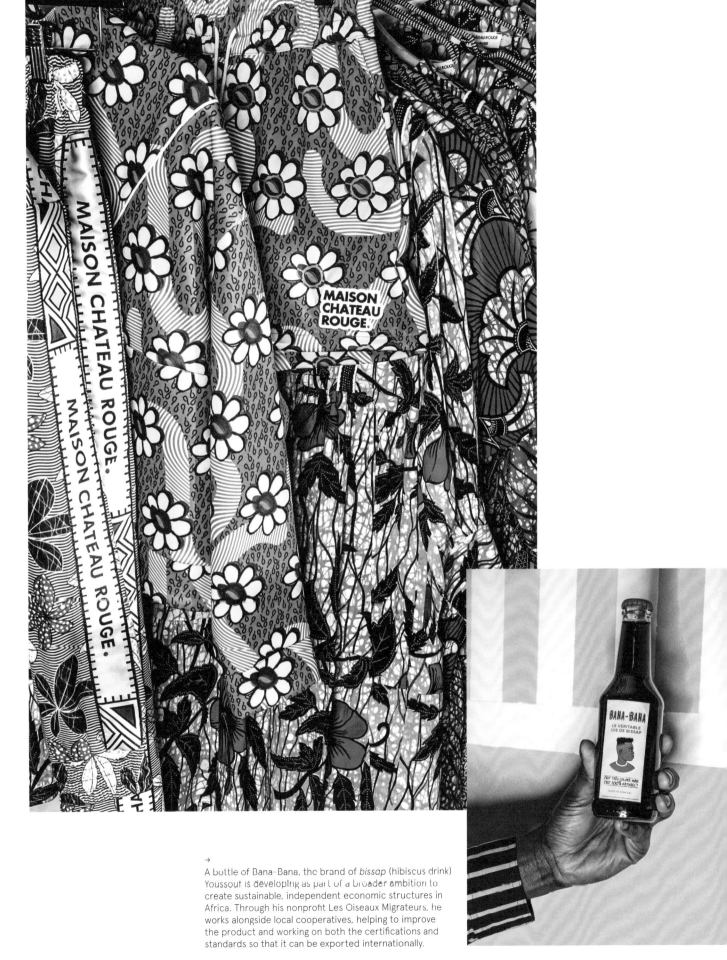

→
A bottle of Bana-Bana, the brand of *bissap* (hibiscus drink) Youssouf is developing as part of a broader ambition to create sustainable, independent economic structures in Africa. Through his nonprofit Les Oiseaux Migrateurs, he works alongside local cooperatives, helping to improve the product and working on both the certifications and standards so that it can be exported internationally.

Youssouf Fofana

VISIT

Maison Château Rouge
40 bis rue Myrha, 75018 Paris
Château Rouge,
METRO: Château Rouge
www.maison-chateaurouge.com

THE NEIGHBORHOOD

The Maison Château Rouge studio and boutique takes its name from, and is located in the heart of, Paris's colorful "Little Africa" quarter. At the foot of Montmartre, in the shadow of Sacré-Coeur, Château Rouge has been an important destination for Paris's African diaspora for decades. A concentration of specialist shops fan out around a fresh food market on the rue Dejean: wax fabric vendors rub shoulders with African tailors; specialist grocers sell everything from Maggi stock cubes to plantain bananas; hardcore halal butchers face off with African seafood markets; black hair and nail salons are located next door to wig and hair-extension specialists. Adding to the chaos, street peddlars sell everything from fresh produce like the *safou*, or African pear, to fake Chanel handbags.

SÉBASTIEN KOPP & FRANÇOIS-GHISLAIN MORILLION

Creative entrepreneurs
Veja

When childhood friends Sébastien and François-Ghislain set up their organic and fair-trade sneaker brand in 2005, they inscribed into its name their commitment to confronting the impact of globalization and to promoting transparency. Veja means "look" in Portuguese, the language of Brazil, the country at the heart of the Veja adventure, where they source their raw materials and have developed unique supply chains in wild rubber and organic cotton.

Frustrated by the cynicism of the companies they were working for as young graduates in management studies, Sébastien and François-Ghislain decided, at just twenty-seven years old, to stop compromising and to set up their own company. They chose to run, so to speak, with the sneaker, a highly conspicuous symbol of consumerism that greatly resonated with their generation. Their first step was to head to the Amazon rainforest where they met with the local rubber tappers (seringueiros) who sustainably harvest the wild latex. Then it was on to northern Brazil to meet with farming coops that produced organic cotton. Next, they upended the traditional business model whereby seventy percent of the price of a pair of sneakers goes to marketing and communication and thirty percent to fabrication. Veja does not advertise, allowing the company to sink those resources into production, raw materials, and the people who make the sneakers. Ever faithful to their founding principles, the friends continue to expend enormous energy to improve their company and its products, but they recognize that "a brand of sneakers—as ecological is it might be, as radical as it might be in its social and economic balance—changes nothing. But it changes us." And that's a good start.

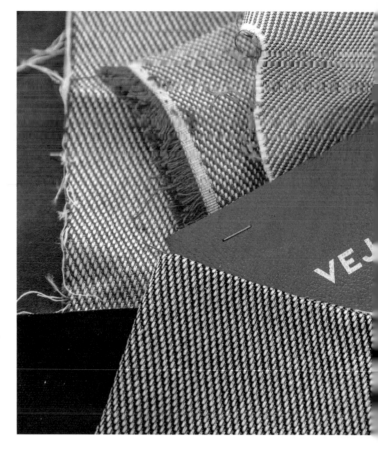

↑
"We started with two supply chains, organic cotton and rubber. And then about five years ago we met people who were making mesh, a more open, breathable fabric, from recycled polyester, recycled plastic bottles. Then we began working on the engineering of our fabrics to try and incorporate more and more organic cotton into our mesh fabrics, because we realized that even if it is recycled, it is still much more ecological to work with a natural and organic material."

←
Contact sheets by the photographer Florent Demarchez who followed François-Ghislain and Sébastien to Brazil in 2007 to meet the seringueiros who harvest the wild latex in the Amazonian rainforest, and the organic cotton producers in Ceará of northeastern Brazil. The resulting photos gave rise to an exhibition Novo Mundo(s) (New World(s)) presented in Paris, Marseille, and London.

↑
"We design with great attention, but we are not really into all the razzle-dazzle of fashion and design: inspirations, mood boards, etc."

↓
"When we launched Veja, there were a few of us with the same idea: to offer well-made clothes or accessories. And I think why we've lasted, the cause of our success, is that we paid as much attention to the production, the materials, and the supply chains, as to the design of the product."

"We like working with latex. We haven't yet succeeded in our dream of making a fully latex sole. We have developed latex cushioning technology, but not an entire sole. It's our dream because we have access to an extraordinary supply chain in the Amazon. Latex is rubber before it is mixed with sulfur. It is the most natural rubber that exists and has excellent properties, its bounce and elasticity are incredible. Latex is really the most noble material of all, that all plastics try to imitate."

Sébastien Kopp & François-Ghislain Morillion

What's a typical day for you?

Today we run a business more than a brand. We're with our teams every day, taking care of others, putting in the energy so that the wheels keep turning. It's no longer just us in a little apartment.

Why Paris?

It's more an era than a place. We are more the fruit of a generation that grew up with globalization, with mass consumption, and at the same time we had access to travel—in any case that's how we really discovered the world, the reality of the world, and its injustices.

What is your motto?

"Transparency above all." Which means just to say what we do; we don't make promises. Because we saw when we worked for big companies that that's how they operate, by writing charters, promises … a bit like politicians, who obviously never respect what they promise. Let's just talk about what is actually done. That's been one of our principles since the beginning.

What do you consider your greatest achievement?

Demonstrating that it's possible to do things differently. Do not moralize, do not give lessons, do not get upset, do not say no, but create and come up with ideas. A brand of sneakers won't change the world, but it can show what is possible. For example, when we discovered the existence of the Fairphone project, they said they were inspired by us. That's quite gratifying. It's times like that when we say to ourselves that if we're of any use at all, it's participating in this reinvention of life.

What inspires you?

An enormous amount of research and development. In the sense that you have to find people doing interesting things. But it requires real research, and travel, and meetings, and that's a lot of our work, finding other people who are "makers," finding a new technology, a new idea, a new way of harvesting. In the end, our purpose, our way of working, is to be alert, so that we can find these people.

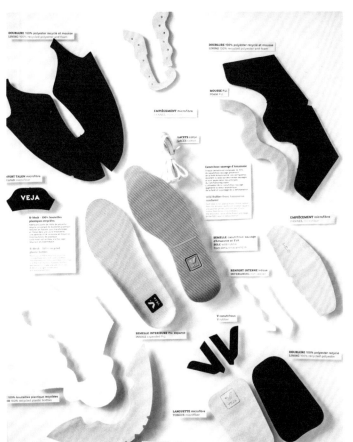

An exploded view of the Veja SDU model, revealing the provenance of every material used. Veja are relentlessly looking to improve every component of their shoes and always to reduce their use of plastics. "We are continually at trade fairs and conferences. We travel constantly to meet people, to be aware of what is under development, and we ourselves are always developing materials." In 2019 they achieved a new milestone with the launch of their first running shoe, the outcome of important investments in research and development.

You won't find Sébastien and François-Ghislain at their desks much. If Sébastien still uses a paper agenda, pretty much every other working tool is digitalized; they work from their laptops. They're nomads.

Sébastien Kopp & François-Ghislain Morillion

VISIT

Centre Commercial
2 rue de Marseille, 75010 Paris
Canal Saint-Martin,
METRO: Jacques Bonsergent
www.centrecommercial.cc

Veja
15 rue de Poitou, 75003 Paris
Northern Marais,
METRO: Filles du Calvaire
www.veja-store.com

THE BOUTIQUE

If Veja is very much a digital brand, with one foot firmly in Brazil, their concept store Centre Commercial provides a local anchor point in Paris, where the company is based. Sébastien, who spent part of his childhood in Marseille, was happy to find a site on the rue de Marseille, a wide, bright street that leads down to the Canal Saint-Martin. Here Veja demonstrates their inclusive spirit of collaboration, bringing together under one roof all sorts of brands, products, and people they love, for a variety of reasons, but with a common trait of "transparency of production; they know where they manufacture, without it necessarily being something they make a big deal out of." On the racks you might find pieces from Parisian workwear brand Bleu de Paname or the pioneering activist company Patagonia. You'll find Veja's latest limited-edition collaboration, as well as a "Made in France" pair from Paraboot. Centre Commercial also hosts regular launches, round tables, exhibitions, and parties. "The idea behind Centre Commercial really was to re-enchant the idea of the shopping center." In late 2019 Veja opened their first boutique worldwide in Paris.

ISAAC REINA

Bag designer
Isaac Reina

After studies in fashion and architecture, Isaac Reina began his career in his native Barcelona as an intern for fashion designer Antonio Miro, which led to a permanent job there. Six years later in 1998, looking for a new challenge, he resigned and followed his French girlfriend to Paris. Three weeks after that, he had a job at one of France's most venerable fashion houses, Hermès, where he worked in menswear. Part of the appeal was that fashion hero Martin Margiela had recently started his role there as artistic director of womenswear.

Hermès introduced Reina to a new level of quality and also to its exceptionally humanistic, family-owned culture where "people have respect and real relationships." From a Protestant family himself, Reina felt an affinity to the house's culture, where "everything is quite simple, not as complicated, not so ostentatious."

In 2006 he left what might have been a long and comfortable career to launch his own label, responding to the personal challenge: "Are you able to do something specific or personal and make it work?" His collections are designed out of a studio and showroom in the Marais, and still handmade in Paris across four separate ateliers, one of which is company owned. "Paris is a place where a tradition of leather exists, like Florence."

Minimalist but not simple, an Isaac Reina bag is a concentration of technical expertise, each one an exquisite exercise in proportion, materials, and manufacturing. Working with generic colors like black, navy, or khaki, the house also regularly explores more subtle, unexpected hues, from a Klein blue to the palest eggshell, as well as textures like an exceptional black patent leather or the finest suede. For smaller leather goods and accessories, Reina likes to work with natural, untreated leather, which develops a beautiful patina with time and wear. Understated, with no hardware and no logo, an Isaac Reina bag is the supreme anti-"It" bag.

↑
"I'm constantly designing. I have a sketchbook with me all the time. I have two or three boxes of them. This is number fifty-six."

Isaac Reina

↑
Isaac Reina designs for other houses too. Six months
after setting up his company, Maison Margiela asked him
to design their handbag collection. "Martin [Margiela]
was always saying that you must go to the limit of a thing.
Not in the middle, you must go to the limit." And more
recently he worked with Raf Simons on the bags for his
short-lived Calvin Klein collab.

↑
"I'm crazy about books. I buy at least two or three
per week. I don't buy much else because I don't like
to own too many things."

These hollow punch cutters serve to cut out the different pieces of leather that comprise each Isaac Reina product. They are custom made by a specialist artisan in the Marais—the only one left in Paris with this expertise.

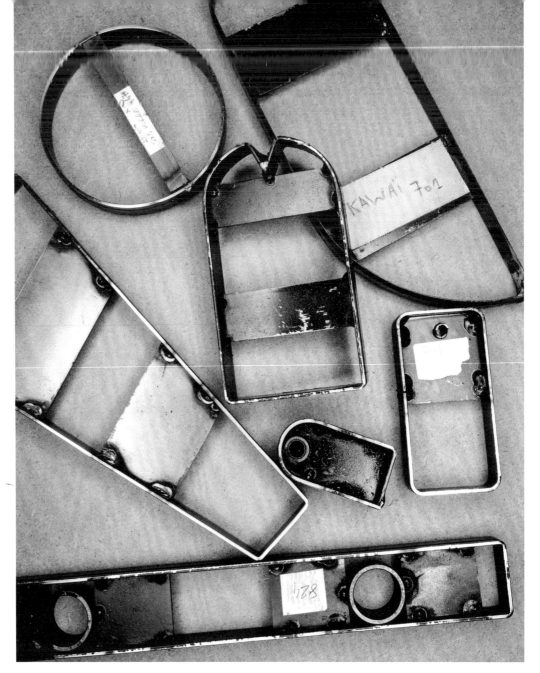

↓
"Each design is drawn to scale by hand, and in the computer. Drawing to scale helps the artisans, who can use it like a pattern."

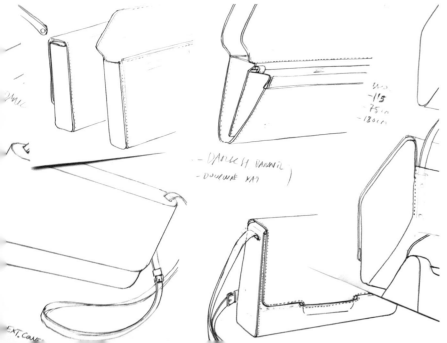

→
A worktable in Isaac Reina's workshop. We see a pattern for the Hitchcock Clutch. Oblong punches, for cutting holes, lie on a cutting board. A fileteuse is an electric machine used for creasing and edging, as well as cauterizing thread ends for a perfect finish.

In true modernist spirit, each model Isaac Reina has ever produced has a reference number—they're into four figures now—but also a name, for example: "N°550. Small Hitchcock bag with strap."

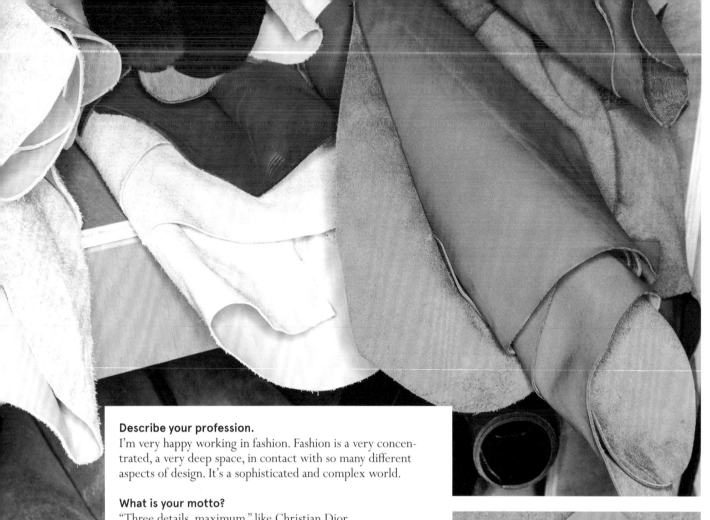

Describe your profession.
I'm very happy working in fashion. Fashion is a very concentrated, a very deep space, in contact with so many different aspects of design. It's a sophisticated and complex world.

What is your motto?
"Three details, maximum," like Christian Dior.

A life-changing meeting?
I started my career working for Antonio Miro in Barcelona. Miro was one of the precursors of minimalism. He influenced me a lot at the beginning. He is an incredible person and the studio was a really crazy place at that time with people like Pedro Almodovar always passing through. For my second job, at Hermès, I was assistant to Véronique Nichanian, the artistic director of the men's department. She has great taste in everything, with an amazing instinct for the right material, the right feel, the right weight. She's an ideal mix of creative, sensitive, and pragmatic.

Why Paris?
It's definitely important where you live and where you work. It's not the same to make films in Hollywood as it is to make films somewhere else. It was important for me to work in Paris just to see what was true and not true, even if Barcelona is a very important place for the Catalan people, for the Spanish people. In the past, during the second half of the last century, many Spanish artists like Picasso, Miró, or Dalí, came to Paris, it was a place of freedom during the dictatorship. So it felt like a very natural place for me to go; it wasn't like going to the end of the world! In terms of culture, Paris is like an infinite sea, with hundreds of cinemas, bookshops, galleries. And for fashion, there are so many different neighborhoods, so many different boutiques, with big houses side by side with small shops. There is a good balance in Paris; in many cities now you only find big chains and big brands.

↑
Reina's pieces are notable for the thinness and suppleness of the leather. Each skin is calibrated using an expensive refining machine, then this manual gauge confirms the thickness, guaranteeing consistency to a tenth of a millimeter across every piece.

→
The 3-D cardboard models of each bag allow the team to visualize each design in space, and in relation to the body.

What inspires you?

I'm constantly inspired by things from daily life and particularly by anonymous, industrial, or generic things. Sometimes quite primitive things. It means I can be anywhere—waiting for somebody, sitting in a bank—and I can be inspired. Usually the process is a very clear translation in leather of a standard thing that has always existed in popular culture, like the brown cardboard folders with elastic closure, things like that. And at the moment I'm often inspired by furniture, by the detail of a piece by Jean Prouvé, or an armchair by Marcel Breuer, for example. The shape of course and by all the little details of how they are made. Because wood is very similar to leather. Another thing that is very important is vintage, maybe because I live very close to the Marché d'Aligre. I go almost every Sunday to the flea market there; if not there, I go to the Saint-Ouen Flea Market (Les Puces de Saint-Ouen). I'm constantly buying vintage leather pieces because they demonstrate techniques that don't exist anymore.

What is luxury?

Leather is expensive and the people that I work with are very experienced, which is expensive too. Also, taxes are high in France. So my work is a little expensive, which is why it might be considered "luxury." But it's not a word that I like, and it's not at all my purpose. On the contrary, I like to make simple, democratic things. I don't like the idea of luxury in terms of separating people, of saying "I'm more elite or more special."

VISIT

Isaac Reina
www.isaacreina.com

20 rue Bonaparte, 75006 Paris
Saint-Germain-des-Prés,
METRO: Saint-Germain-des-Prés

12 rue de Thorigny, 75003 Paris
Marais, METRO: Saint-Sébastien-Froissart

THE NEIGHBORHOOD

Isaac Reina opened a second shop in Saint-Germain in 2018. All the shop's display units, the stairwell, and the checkout area are sheathed in natural leather that develops a deep patina over time. A collaboration with the Belgian architect Bernard Dubois, the Saint-Germain boutique is a rich iteration of the house's identity and philosophy that Isaac is proud of. He loves the neighborhood too. "Saint-Germain has an amazing vibe, with all the antique shops and the fine arts school (École des Beaux-Arts) at the end of the street—one of the first art schools in the world! I discovered that Eileen Gray lived her whole life in an apartment across the street, at 21 rue Bonaparte—an amazing place, look it up on Google. Charlotte Perriand lived on rue Bonaparte too, close to the church...."

BENOÎT ASTIER DE VILLATTE & IVAN PERICOLI

Designers
Astier de Villatte

Inspired by overlooked treasures they unearth in flea markets, find abandoned in the street, or perhaps dig out of the back of a cupboard at their grandmother's, the Paris design company Astier de Villatte are famous for their beautiful collections of white tableware—ceramic follies that for the most part seem teleported out of an imagined pre-industrial age, or from the decadent tables of a European aristocracy now falling into ruin. "Château cheap" is how Ivan, one half of the duo that comprises the company, describes their unique style.

If the company carries Benoît's family name it's because their beginnings were very much the outgrowth of his family's culture. Benoit's father is the painter Pierre Carron, who taught at the École des Beaux-Arts for over thirty years. "There was a kiln in my father's studio, so it was very simple for us to be able to make plates and things, it happened quite naturally. I think our first pieces came out of his studio."

Benoît and Ivan met while students at the École des Beaux-Arts, where their taste for still lifes clashed with the dogma of the day that declared figurative art to be dead. When they wanted to paint or draw, or visit the Louvre, they were considered freaks—"the other students came to visit us like at the zoo." But they stayed true to their muse and launched Astier de Villatte with Benoît's older siblings a few years later in 1996.

The breadth of their vision became fully apparent with the opening of their own boutique on the rue Saint-Honoré in 2004, a perfectly decrepit space that had been closed and untouched for years before they moved in. An equally beautiful second boutique opened on the Left Bank in 2016. While their pottery takes center stage, Benoît and Ivan orchestrate an infinitude of intoxicating atmospheres. Their collection of scented candles conjure places at once dreamed and real, from Hollywood to Marienbad and the Palais de Tokyo to the Villa Medici. Their dishwashing liquids are perfumed with pepper and bergamot. Their eaux de colognes are sold in hand-blown glass bottles made in Florence, and their incense sticks are made on the Japanese island of Awaji using ancestral techniques. Printed in one of Paris's last remaining letterpress printers, now owned by Astier de Villatte, their stylish diaries have become must-have items. Everywhere one's gaze alights, a thrilling new composition materializes.

↑
Most of the fifty or so craftsmen working for Astier de Villatte are political refugees fleeing oppression in their native Tibet, and many are former or actual Buddhist monks. Benoît thinks their philosophical and spiritual education partly explains the very special atmosphere that reigns in the workshop. And Ivan explains that there's also a rare relationship between employer and employee based on trust: "So we are never telling them to hurry up, or produce more; that vocabulary does not exist. There are words that are never said in the workshop."

←
The black terracotta and the soft slab molding, or *estampage*, technique that Astier de Villatte use to make their pottery collections was inherited from one of their professors at the École des Beaux-Arts in Paris, the sculptor Georges Jeanclos.

←

To make each Astier de Villatte piece, a slab of rolled-out clay is carefully molded in or on one of the ceramic concave "slump" or convex "hump" molds. It's tempting to make parallels between these techniques and the Tibetan Buddhism practice of the Torma, sometimes elaborate ritual cakes typically sculpted out of flour and butter that embody Buddhist concepts of selflessness and impermanence.

↑

All Astier de Villatte ceramics are one hundred percent made in Paris. The company headquarters are located about halfway between the French National Library and the Boulevard Péripherique in the 13th arrondissement, a popular, former industrial neighborhood. Inside a modern, multi-story office building there, all production stages are carried out on the ground floor, across the workshop, packing and shipment areas, while upstairs is the office.

→→

The bisque-fired pieces after a first passing in the kiln. They are now ready to be glazed.

→→→

The finished pieces for sale in the shop. Astier de Villatte's irregular white glaze is the house's signature, small imperfections reveal the dark clay beneath, underscoring the pieces' handmade quality and giving them a very special charm.

Benoît Astier de Villatte & Ivan Pericoli

Describe your profession.

B: When we started to see that we were being described as ceramists—ceramics is a very serious and technical profession, you have to know many things that we did not know—we proclaimed ourselves designers.

What's a typical day for you?

I: We are at the office a lot. The drama of designers is that you are in the office a lot doing everything except design.

B: In general we are in the workshop during the day; when Setsuko is there we spend time with her. We are always circulating in the workshop, solving problems, being present.

What is unique about your work?

I: What's interesting when you read a beautiful novel is that all of a sudden you are immersed in an atmosphere, you are transported somewhere. I think that's exactly what we want to do at Astier de Villatte, to transport people to a fairly undefined somewhere else. A past that did not exist, a bizarre future; you don't know where you are. We like to conjure atmospheres. When we present each new collection to the press, we like to create spaces that resemble a seedy hotel like you might find in an Agatha Christie novel.

What inspires you?

I: We come from a fine arts background. We grew up in artists' studios. Everyone was wanting to do contemporary art, and we wanted to paint and draw. And to do that, we needed props, because we worked from nature. So we'd walk out on to rue Bonaparte and we'd find a table on the street, and we'd take it. Then you have to put something on it, so we picked up something else in the trash, or we'd bring an old piece of fabric from home, that could be used in our still lifes.

What is luxury?

B: I think it's about wanting to do the best you can. To give yourself the means to do the best you can. Of course, that results in products that are expensive. So unfortunately it's addressed to a customer who can afford to pay, but it's not the desire to make expensive products. It's that the products are expensive because the process is expensive.

What is your favorite neighborhood in Paris?

I: The Paris flea market is one of the most interesting places in the world. It's a fabulous treasure that could disappear at any moment, because people don't buy antiques anymore. I think the way to relaunch the Puces is with an environmental argument. There is nothing more ecofriendly than buying second-hand clothes and furniture. And most of the time it's cheaper than IKEA.

B: And what's more, I think there's something romantic in the sense that, if you like, you're in your little box—your house—and then you wonder, How to escape? How to create something in this box? Of course, by opening a book—a novel gets us out of there—but also by going to the flea market, you can create something in this white box. You can very easily introduce a small portrait, and all of a sudden you are in an almost fictional world. Or you don't want a portrait, you want something more modern. The themes are infinite. Like in the theater.

Why Paris?

I: I almost always have the same conversation with taxi drivers—when they're not complaining about the demonstrations, the roadworks, or the mayor. I like to talk with them about how lucky they are to work in Paris. It's one of the splendid cities.

↑
When asked to choose an emblematic piece, Ivan responds that no single object could represent their house, that it must be an ensemble: a silver-glazed jug (the silver glazing is very difficult to achieve); their very personal guide to Paris, *Ma Vie à Paris*; an incense holder designed by the sculptor Serena Carone; and the cat teapot designed by their friend Setsuko Klossowska de Rola, a particular favorite of Ivan's ("I love cats; I have three.").

→ Benoît was born in Rome when his artist father Pierre Carron was a fellow at the Villa Medici, while the painter Balthus was director there. Today Balthus's widow Setsuko Klossowska de Rola is an important collaborator with the house. She still lives high up in the Swiss alps in the historic Grand Chalet she shared with Balthus, their children, and their cats, but regularly comes to work with them in the Paris workshop. She has designed many ceramic pieces for Astier de Villatte, and they have also worked together on distilling the Grand Chalet's scent, an enchanting smell inspired by the ancient linden tree that shades the garden there. While "Atelier de Balthus" evokes the painter's studio, fragrant with the heady smell of turpentine, Dunhill cigarettes, and cedar wood.

Astier de Villatte
www.astierdevillatte.com

173 rue Saint-Honoré, 75001 Paris
Louvre, METRO: Palais Royal-Musée
du Louvre

16 rue de Tournon, 75006 Paris
Left Bank, METRO: Odéon

FLASHBACK

"We started out at the Viaduc des Arts, under the arches on Avenue Daumesnil. We had a studio there, where lots of dust fell in the window, which was disgusting. From time to time we ate on the sidewalk when it was nice weather, and Parisians would pass by with their strollers and would ask, 'How much is this cup you have in the window?' 'Fifty euros,' we'd reply. 'Thief! Asshole!' they would cry. We were insulted all day long. So we got fed up and stopped answering people. Then we ended up finding an old shop on rue Saint-Honoré and there we have rarely been yelled at."

Benoît Astier de Villatte & Ivan Pericoli —

JAMES HEELEY

Perfumer
Heeley

Niche perfumer James Heeley came to the world of scent via a meandering journey that took him from studies in philosophy and law to graphic, product, and furniture design before gradually circling in, like a bee to a flower, on perfume.

Born and raised in Yorkshire, James read philosophy and law at King's College London before coming to Paris for a year around the early 1990s, with an inquisitive mind and creative inclinations. He never went back to law. Instead, he began running with a group of art school grads in Paris who had an advertising agency, where he worked on graphic design projects and learned about typesetting, packaging, and lots in between. He also set up a studio in the Père Lachaise neighborhood where he "was welding and making furniture and just experimenting." Inspired by an artisan working near his studio who was repairing antique zinc planters, James began crafting vases out of this material, its iconic silvery-blue sheen so familiar from Parisian rooftops. He was soon selling his vases at Christian Tortu, the star Paris florist of the day, and so began an enduring collaboration throughout the mid-to-late 1990s that eventually brought James into the world of scent.

Work on an interior scent project with Christian Tortu and Annick Goutal introduced James to the technical reality of perfume making. It was a revelation when he "realized there was a whole creative process behind scent" that resonated with his taste for crafting complete aesthetic worlds. An ongoing relationship with a lab near the town of Grasse provided the resources to build his scent vocabulary and technical know-how, and in 2001 he launched a range of scented candles; five years later, his first perfume, Menthe Fraîche, was born.

As the creator of one of Europe's few independent perfume houses, James has rare freedom to express his own vision and imagination. Each of his fragrances are elegant exercises in style—contemporary, unisex perfumes that each distill small truths from nature.

↑
A detail of a recipe of one of James's perfumes that typically contain around thirty different ingredients, though he's always looking to simplify. "The basic skeleton of the perfume is usually done relatively quickly, because that's just instant 'I like it or I don't.' But then to really get it, get the balance and get it to really work as a perfume, that takes a bit more time. You have to sometimes smell it then go back to it; it can grow on you or feel too obvious or not really interesting."

→
Trials of formulated perfume, neither macerated or matured, and part of the ping pong with the lab involved in developing each new composition. "This idea of setting up as a perfumer with droppers, etc., is a complete fantasy, it wouldn't work, it's too laborious. In the lab where I work, there's a machine, Roxane, that contains one hundred raw materials that make up maybe seventy percent of the formula; you can send the formula directly to Roxane digitally, then the remaining raw materials that make up that formula are weighed physically."

↑
Vials of raw materials—the essences that make up the finished product—
including one of James's favorite scents, Haitian vetiver. This scent is used in
many of his compositions, including Vetiver Veritas, his only entirely natural
perfume. "It is not that easy to create 100 percent natural perfume, to make it
work, and there are very, very few on the market. Vetiver Veritas is actually the
perfume I made for myself. Through making it I realized that the great difference between naturals and synthetics is that naturals are far more complex."

James Heeley 89

What is unique about your work?

I guess all perfumers are autodidacts, like painters used to be. You don't become a perfumer after going to perfume school. The only way you can make perfume is actually to do it. It's a bit like playing the guitar; it's not because you've been to music school that you're a good guitarist.

Your style?

Most of my perfumes have a very natural feel and they tend to be sort of light and optimistic, and always quite well-balanced. They're quite subtle. They have a very natural, elegant feel to them I think.

Describe your profession.

It's a little like painting, cooking, and music. There are similarities between many different creative processes. For example, in painting you mix primary colors to get more complex colors. It's the same in scent, you can use raw materials to build other raw materials, to get other smells. All scents are an assemblage of accords. You can get grapefruit by combining lemon and mandarin for example, and you can make rose or something near it without using rose. There's no extract of, say, lily of the valley; rather, it's constructed around jasmine with green notes. And that's when it becomes a bit like music: you have notes, compositions of high notes, low notes, round notes. Or it's almost visual, described as vivid colors or dark colors or textures. And all that is part of your olfactory memory, or your creative baggage. How you remember scents and what they project, what ideas they stimulate.

Why Paris?

I went out with a French girl at university and I came to Paris and I really liked it. And at the time I was wanting to get away from London and change direction. I qualified as a barrister when I was twenty-one and I didn't feel ready at all, so I thought I'm going to take a year out, go to Paris, and see what happens. And it was just so much easier to live here and get by without much money. At the same time, I was learning a new language, I was learning new things. It was very stimulating and I felt free here. And I still do, and I still feel a bit like a stranger. I like that feeling of being a foreigner in a country that I know well enough to get around in but where I'm not part of the furniture.

↑
Two of James's zinc vases that he
designed and made for the florist
Christian Tortu in the 1990s. "For me
it's the beginning because it's the
first time I was designing profession-
ally. I thought he was the best florist
at the time, it was the only place
I really wanted to exhibit my vases.
It was such an exciting period for me.
I worked on some fantastic design
projects for Andrée Putman and
was encouraged by some wonderful clients like Luminaire in Miami,
Maxfield in LA, and of course, Colette
here in Paris."

→
A refreshing whiff of sun, sand, and
sea air. "Sel Marin is probably the
most iconic of the perfumes. The
idea is you smell of the sea. It wasn't
the earliest but it's definitely the one
that, along with Cardinal, put us on
the map." The bottle sits in one of
James's Sono vases, his original packaging for the perfume and scented
candles. Handmade from multiple
layers of high-density foam and cut
to form watertight blocks, it can be
recycled as a vase or pot.

VISIT

Heeley
34 galerie de Montpensier,
Jardin du Palais Royal,
75001 Paris
Palais-Royal, METRO: Palais Royal–
Musée du Louvre
www.jamesheeley.com

THE LOCATION
James opened his first shop in 2019, choosing to set up under
the arcades of the Palais-Royal. "I love being in a garden.
I've traveled a lot and I've never seen another old building that
was actually designed around a garden and shops in its original conception. I think it's very rare. There's some inconve-
niences; it gets really dusty because of the sand for example.
But it's typically Parisian. And it's the side of Paris that I really
like. When I first came to Paris I never really got the difference
between the Left and Right Bank, and now I totally get that.
And I'm much happier on the Right Bank; as an environment
it's just more connected."

James Heeley —

MAJID
MOHAMMAD

Florist
Muse

In his Montmartre flower shop, Majid Mohammad has created a little sanctuary where the beauty of the natural world fuses with civilization's splendors. He orchestrates a magical moment in time with the colors and forms of flowers and plants, their scents, their delicate freshness. Interspersed amongst the flowers are antiques, vases, sculptures, and art tomes. Classical music booms from the speakers.

Born and raised in Tehran, Majid trained and worked as an accountant before the country's mounting fundamentalism made life increasingly difficult. "I worked for an organization that was linked to the government. I was fired, because you had to wear a beard, you had to pray, you had to wear certain clothes, and that didn't suit me. Psychologically, it became very painful." A family friend who owned a couple of flower shops shops in Tehran asked Majid to help out. "It's hard to explain, but it's like it was waiting for me, unconsciously this had always been my true profession."

In the early 2000s, at thirty years old, Majid immigrated to France with his family where he had to learn not just a new language and culture, but also a rich, new floral vocabulary. He also discovered that in Paris, floristry is practically an extension of the fashion industry; its cycles follow the fashion week calendar as much as nature's seasons. Four times a year the city's florists are called upon to decorate showrooms, prepare gift bouquets for favorite journalists or influencers, and perhaps even decorate the show venues.

As well as fashion week—working with Maison Margiela or Jean-Paul Gaultier, for example—Majid's busy working life is ordered around three weekly trips to the market to restock. He gets up at 3 or 4 a.m. and drives his van out to Rungis, the world's largest fresh produce market, located on the outskirts of Paris, to make his selection and renew his immersion in life's seasons and cycles.

←
Majid has a large and varied collection of vases that he has picked up here and there. "I often go to the Saint-Ouen Flea Market. I love this place. It's like an open-air museum, but even better, because you can touch everything."

↓
In the place of a till an antique Chinoiserie cabinet. "I picked it up at the Braderie de Lille flea market. I think it was made around 1800. I'm not sure if it is of Chinese or Japanese inspiration, it's a bit of a mix."

In his approach to his shop display, Majid thinks in terms of color, organizing the flowers according to hue or texture, and presenting them in a cacophony of different vases; clear glass, which lets you see the stems, among flashes of glazed ceramic, lacquer-work, and brass.

Why do you work where you do?

I love Montmartre, it's a bit removed from the rest of Paris. I love that it sits atop the rest of the city. The neighborhood has an inspiring, bohemian history, on which so many artists have left their mark.

What profession other than your own would you like to try?

If I had to change professions, I would be happy being an antique dealer. I love decoration and decorative objects.

What is luxury?

Luxury is having time, which I never have. But having flowers in every room is pretty special too.

What inspires you?

Paintings inspire me—and not just paintings of flowers—by the atmosphere they can convey, and how they can immortalize a moment in time. Like a bouquet that as it fades reveals time's passing. Nature, that divine creation, is also a great source of inspiration. I let nature play its role in my flower arrangements, but not too much either; at times I intervene to add my personal touch.

What is unique about your work?

I think that the sensibility that I communicate in my floral compositions stands out from the crowd. I think my compositions tell a story, when looked at poetically. I transmit emotion, and that's difficult. Not everyone can do it. To work with your hands but create something with spirit is extremely subtle and sensitive work.

A life-changing meeting?

For many years I have been working for a world famous fashion designer, the creative director of Maison Margiela. I am honored to work for this great artist. Flowers are important to him. By giving me freedom to express myself, he pushes me to create new things.

"I like things that are pretty messy, I like very generous things, very baroque, very colorful; and I like to leave the flowers free in the composition." Majid's dramatic bouquets often include arching or hanging stems or branches, and perfumed flowers too, perhaps sweet pea, rose, or tuberose. "I buy a lot of French flowers, it's important. Ecuador and Kenya are big producers of roses, but I don't buy those because they have traveled such a long way; they're full of chemicals and pesticides—they never really die—and they smell bad. I only buy roses when they are in season, in spring and summer, from a producer I know. The seasons are one of the joys of the trade."

VISIT

Muse
4 rue Burq, 75018 Paris
Montmartre, METRO: Abbesses
Instagram: @musemontmartre

Majid Mohammad —

SIGOLÈNE PRÉBOIS & CATHERINE LÉVY

Designers
Tsé & Tsé Associées

Colorful paper garlands, wonky white porcelain plates and cups, delicate string lights, articulated lamps, constellations of mismatched vases.... Tsé & Tsé's designs for interiors are as whimsical and charming as the duo that designs them. Sigolène Prébois and Catherine Lévy met as teenagers, two misfits from posh neighborhoods of Paris who liked making their own clothes. After high school, the friends enrolled together at ENSCi, a new experimental industrial design school "where you don't teach" but rather practice, established under the patronage of French design legends Jean Prouvé and Charlotte Perriand. The hands-on, "design-for-all" spirit that reigned there soon manifested into a collective Sigolène and Catherine formed with another student, Renaud Supiot, called Braguette Magique. The trio made wild latex jewelry—"fat, rubbery, pink, blue, spotty, and striped hedgehogs, mice, elephants and spermatozoids"—that were sold in shops around town, bringing them a certain notoriety and a taste for independence.

←
"It's true that our structure, our way of working, the fact that we manufacture and distribute ourselves is only possible because we have a place of this size. It's funny, we didn't choose this independence. At first, we thought it was how we could prove what we could do, and after that we would work as designers. But then we tasted this freedom, and that's really the word for it. We always have the impression that we are in a little boat, in a walnut shell, but at the same time, it's our boat!"

→
"We were inspired by test tubes for this vase. Today it looks so familiar, you have the impression you've seen it before. But at the time, it seemed to come from another planet! No one understood what it would look like with flowers in it. It was perceived as crude, more like a technical object."

They formed Tsé & Tsé Associées soon after graduating, and not long after that, in 1992, their first creation was born. April Vase is a string of twenty-one test tubes linked together by zinc bands whose industrial aesthetic suggests an ikebana-esque poetry once filled with flowers. The florist Christian Tortu understood the vase's beauty and bought out their first stock for his cult Saint-Germain-des-Prés boutique. Influential design gallery Sentou picked it up soon after, and since then April Vase has become Tsé & Tsé's bestseller, a design classic now held in the collection of the Centre Pompidou.

Decades later, Tsé & Tsé Associées have come up with many more useful, beautiful, and somehow inevitable pieces that cheer our lives. They have remained an independent company that designs, manufactures, and distributes their own creations, all from a huge old factory tucked away behind the Place de la Bastille.

↑
"There is almost no room on the shelves where for twenty-five years we have accumulated everything we like and that could be a source of inspiration for creating new objects. We really love rummaging around flea markets—for ideas as much as for objects. We wander around with our eyes popping out of our heads. Travel is less interesting today, with globalization; now we travel through time. It amounts to the same thing."

Sigolène Prébois & Catherine Lévy

"Perriand, a master. She saw our April Vaco and sent us a wonderful letter of congratulations."

CHARLOTTE PERRIAND
UN ART DE VIVRE
Musée des Arts Décoratifs / Flammarion

Against the back wall of the studio sits a composition of vintage work-shop drawer units they salvaged from a neighbor of their former studio, an artisan who made numbered plates of the kind still fixed to the exterior. Today the "drawers are full of treasures that we may never have the opportunity to use."

→ The door to their show-room, where for each new season they present their collections to buyers and the press. "There are periods, seasons: Christmas, the trade fairs in September; Our pieces need to be ready at that time. And we have to think about how we will present these objects too, with what images, because that's how they are chosen, loved, and understood."

What is unique about your work?
What is special is that we use our own creations every day: our cups to drink our tea, our vases to arrange our flowers, our lamps to shed light.

Is there a secret to your job?
Yes, sincerity. We've never designed an object without wanting it for ourselves.

Describe your workshop.
Our workshop is located in a beautiful brick building dating from the late-nineteenth century, where light floods in. Our studio is very tidy—we have space to work, the tables are clear—and at the same time very cluttered.

Why do you work where you do?
We've been in this neighborhood since our studies; our design school wasn't very far away. It's historically the furniture manufacturing district of Paris. But the real reason for our attachment to this part of Paris is the proximity to the Place d'Aligre where almost every morning there's a flea market that we love to scour and a multicultural food market where we do all our food shopping.

What do you consider your greatest achievement?
The April Vase, a poetic creation.

What is your greatest extravagance?
Continuing to have faith.

A life-changing meeting?
The two of us.

↑
Tsé & Tsé assemble their products themselves. When the different pieces come back from the various manufacturers they are quality controlled and assembled here. Furniture is stained and varnished. All the lamps are wired, using the electrical cable on the right. A constellation of their ceramic *Cornettes* lamps hang above the table.

↑
Tsé & Tsé's work process is like a game of ping-pong, with ideas flying back and forth between the two designers. The early stages are less about drawing than making: tests, models, prototypes.... There is a lot of research. The idea is not to fully develop the design at first, but to keep an open and creative mind when talking to the manufacturer, as sometimes there are compromises. "We don't decide that it will be super beautiful like that and that it can't change an iota; design for us is about adapting, working against a constraint, and finding the right solution."

↑
Sigolène's workbench.

Sigolène Prébois & Catherine Lévy

VISIT

Tsé & Tsé Associées
7 rue Saint-Roch, 75001 Paris
Louvre, METRO: Tuileries
www.tse-tse.com

THE NEIGHBORHOOD
"Rue Saint-Roch is a street with beautiful light, there's always sun. We have the Church of Saint-Roch on one side of our boutique, and the Tuileries on the other, it's extraordinary. When we were looking for a space to rent, our friends Astier de Villatte, whose boutique is not far away, recommended the neighborhood, as there's a bit of everything, real Parisians and tourists. We like it a lot."

Sigolène Prébois & Catherine Lévy —

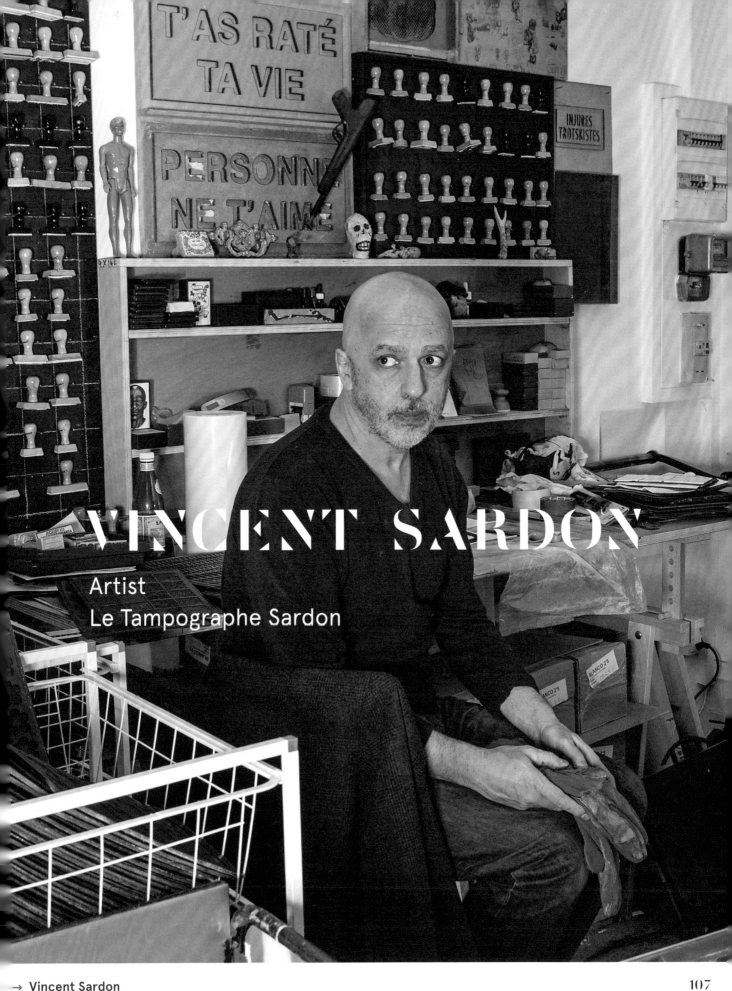

VINCENT SARDON

Artist
Le Tampographe Sardon

↑
"My inspiration comes from a variety of worlds that have been around me since childhood: a certain style of absurd French art, fine arts, decorative arts, literature, we can mix in popular culture too, and the dregs of ordinary culture. A mix of everything."

Using rubber stamps as his medium, Vincent Sardon expresses a dark, cynical take on the human condition, alleviated with sustained flashes of mordant humor, ridiculous smut, and simple beauty. Just add an "ic" to the end of his surname and you pretty much get his job description. Each stamp functions like a small vanitas, a futile but hopefully entertaining act of resistance against the transience of life.

A trained illustrator, Vincent studied art at university in Bordeaux. Immersion in the culture of comics and graphic novels in his free time provided a master class in the art of combining dark themes with humor. At twenty-five years old, he published his first graphic novel *Nénéref*, a short collection of vignettes devoted to dead writers, imagining everyone from Jean-Paul Sartre to Charles Bukowski in improbable and droll scenarios. The same year, 1995, he took the train to Paris. "When I arrived in Paris there was a kind of effervescence in the domain of indie and micro publishing, fanzines, graphics ... there were a lot of things going on, it was a pretty exciting time for me. There were a lot of illustrators, we showed each other our work, we hung out together, there was rivalry nevertheless, which made me progress artistically."

In 1998 and 2000 he published two more graphic novels, this time with the influential underground comic book publisher L'Association, and around the same time he began working as an illustrator for the French left wing daily *Libération*. His final collaboration with them on 18 January 2008 (before moving on to work at *Le Monde*), showed President Sarkozy dancing around the newspaper's cover. He composed Sarko's articulated figure using a series of stamps—a different one for each limb and the head. Indeed, his first-ever stamps, carved out of simple erasers, were a shortcut he improvised to avoid drawing the same character over and over again.

While working for *Le Monde*, Vincent had been quietly developing his stamp art. "I noticed that when I showed my stamps to people something happened, but when I showed my drawings on French politics or the socialist party, it was clearly a flat line on an EEG ... I went towards what seemed to work." In 2007 he participated in a group show at the Musée des Arts Décoratifs in Paris called *Toy Comix*. He also launched his blog—today superseded by an online shop and Instagram account, building a cult following worldwide through the far reach of social media. Then in 2010 he took the leap and stopped working for *Le Monde* to dedicate himself full-time to his stamp art. Today you can meet the artist and experience full immersion in his uniquely dark but playful imagination in the boutique gallery—open to the public on Saturdays—then walk it off at the Père-Lachaise cemetery next door.

↑

Vincent runs his business with his partner Eva (and their fox terrier Olga). Here she stands in a corner of their boutique gallery, which is open to customers on Saturdays only. The rest of the week, they're in the lab, in production mode. Le Tampographe Sardon designs, manufactures, and distributes. "We prefer to control everything because it seems to us the healthiest model on several levels: creatively, in terms of the distribution, the prices, and for the relationship to the customer. It is not even a choice, in fact, it is the only solution."

→

Vincent is constantly sketching and trying out new ideas. "When an idea comes to me and it makes me laugh, I know it will make other people laugh too." Smut often makes him smile. "Handcrafted by an authentic Parisian neurotic" is proudly stamped on every label.

→→

Vincent uses brayers, a traditional printmaking tool, to apply ink or paint to his giant stamps that are too big for any ink pad.

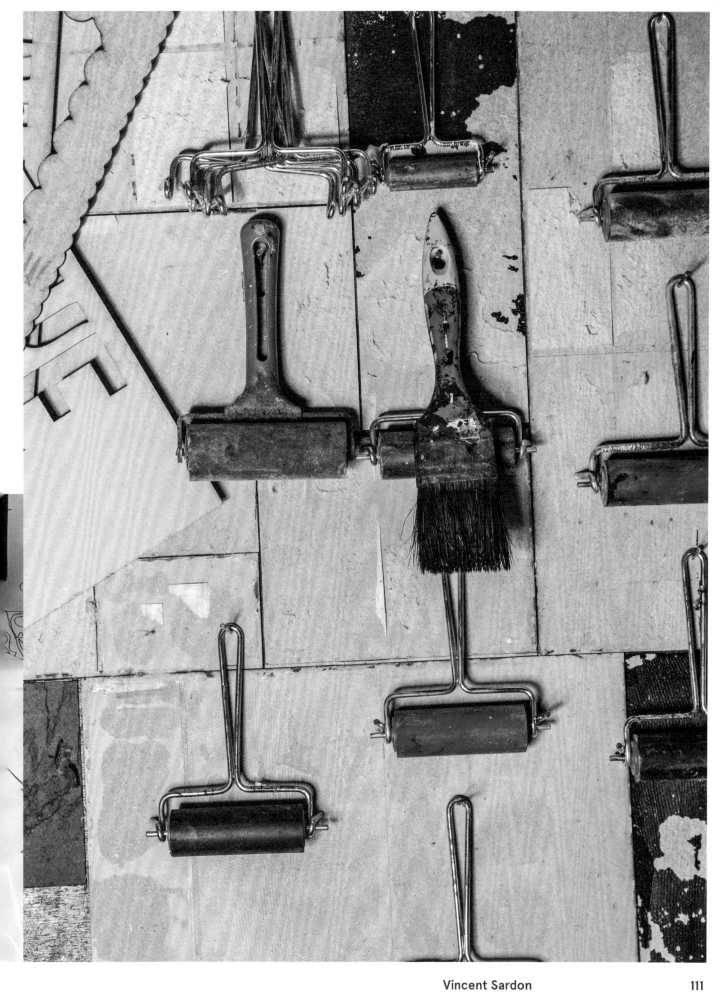

↑
Here Vincent holds a number of his polychrome stamps, notably a human heart and a Mexican-inspired skull. Stamp printing "is a very simple printing process that nevertheless allows you to make some pretty complicated things; quite unexpected things compared to what we imagine to be the possibilities of the stamp."

→
"We are also conditioned by hundreds of years of bureaucracy. So we tend to bestow an almost magical power on the stamp. When we write something stupid with a stamp, it takes on a stronger magical dimension. And if you write something on a gift card, for example, you won't perceive it the same way as if you write it on a Post-it. It's this kind of thing that interests me."

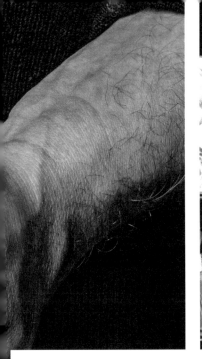

What is unique about your work?
Quite a few things. I have invented a profession of sorts that combines artistic creation, craft, business, writing, and jokes of questionable taste.

What is your greatest extravagance?
Keeping my quirky business alive in a city as inhospitable as Paris.

What's a typical day for you?
Ten hours a day, six days a week: lab, studio, computer, greeting customers, emails, chores of all sorts, with plenty of coffee and fits of hysterics that serve as breaks.

Do you have a motto?
Vivement qu'on soit morts, or "Bring on death." I painted this on a plate and hung it in my kitchen.

Who is your hero?
José Guadalupe Posada. He was an artist and printer who distributed his work himself. On a different note, I like the DIY approach of Jack White and his label Third Man Records. He's pushed things to a new level of perfection.

A life-changing meeting?
Jean-Christophe Menu, the first real publisher who discovered me, published my first book, and helped the Tampographe ("Stampographer") make a name for himself.

What is unique about Paris?
A mix of poignant beauty and the smell of garbage, which gives it its own distinctive tang.

What is your favorite neighborhood in Paris?
The second arrondissement, around the rue Sainte-Anne. For the Japanese restaurants, the covered passageways, and the shadows of the Palais-Royal arches when the sun is shining.

What is luxury?
A status symbol used by a disgusting class to distinguish itself from the rest of the population.

↑
Every item purchased at the shop is wrapped in a brown paper bag and decorated with one of Vincent's creations chosen especially for each customer. Here Vincent composes his dreamy "Rooftops of Paris" with eleven separate stamps.

LE TAMPOGRAPHE SARDON

VISIT

Le Tampographe Sardon
4 rue du Repos, 75020 Paris
Père-Lachaise,
METRO: Philippe Auguste
www.letampographe.bigcartel.com

MUST BUY

With a simple flip of the middle finger, contempt, protest, provocation, resistance, or rage are communicated with perfect economy, the message instantly crossing national borders, language, and time. Already popular in ancient Greece and known as *digitus impudicus* in ancient Rome, the "impudent finger" has to be humankind's oldest insulting gesture. The Tampographe appropriates it for one of Sardon's most popular stamps, the first he made after learning how to produce stamps from photographs. It's exceptionally satisfying to use.

Vincent Sardon –

SOPHIE & DOMINIQUE SENNELIER

Art supply merchants
Sennelier

Sophie Sennelier, herself an artist, took over her family's historic art supply store In 2006 when her father, Dominique, retired. For over a century, from a magic site with views across the Seine to the Louvre, a stone's throw from Paris's Ecole des Beaux-Arts, the Sennelier family has nurtured a rare relationship with artists—including masters like Picasso, Degas, and Cézanne—working hand in hand with them to develop and source the tools and the colors they need to express their creative vision.

The fabulous story of this four-generation family business is inseparable from the history of Paris and of its artists, as well as a cluster of scientific and political developments that took place in the nineteenth century when Paris was the artistic capital of the world. Advances in chemistry at the time produced the first synthetic hues, extending the painter's palette for the first time since the Renaissance. Technological innovation also gave rise to the portable paint tube, allowing painters to get out of their studios to freely experiment with these dazzling new colors. Added to this was the upheaval of the old social order following the industrial revolution as a flourishing bourgeoisie embraced the arts, with, for example, many well-brought-up young ladies now taught to draw and dabble in watercolor.

Sennelier opened in 1887 when Gustave Sennelier, a chemist, took over a bankrupt color merchant on the Left Bank. The Impressionist movement was in full swing by then and a newly specialized trade in pigments flourished alongside. According to Sennelier, in 1817 there were seventy-nine color merchants; by 1885 there were six hundred. Right from the start, Gustave had an advantage: trained in chemistry, he was not simply a reseller but a manufacturer. He sourced his raw materials far and wide, then ground them on a granite table at the back of the shop before preparing the final product for sale. For over a century, Sennelier has contributed to the history of art, developing new tones like Hélios Red, perfecting compositions by, for example, adding honey to their watercolors, or developing revolutionary new media such as professional-grade oil pastels.

← Blue is the rarest natural pigment on earth. Prior to its synthesis in a laboratory in the eighteenth century, painters had to buy powdered lapis lazuli, a semi-precious stone that rivaled the price of gold. The first modern synthetic pigment was *Bleu de Prusse*, or Prussian Blue, developed by a German chemist in the early eighteenth century. About a century later a French chemist developed *Bleu Outremer*, or Ultramarine; other synthesized blues, such as Cobalt Blue, appeared around the same time. Artists could now freely experiment with the color.

The first pigments man ever used to paint were dug out of the earth. Man's earliest creative urges, tens of thousands of years old, survive on cave walls: lions, mammoths, or woolly rhinoceroses sketched in a paste made from ochre, sienna, or umber. Artists continue to use these powders to make their own paints today.

↑
In addition to paint tubes, Sennelier began selling large pots of their excellent water-based paint at the request of the avant-garde Parisian artist Sonia Delaunay, who needed large quantities to cover, for example, the surfaces of her famous *Rythmes-Couleurs* series. Sennelier started filling empty jam jars with their gouache especially for her, and now this format is a permanent fixture of their catalog.

Sophie & Dominique Sennelier

What is unique about your work?
We are proud to have worked in collaboration with artists for four generations. That relationship is what's interesting. It is what excites us the most.

What is your favorite tool?
We are the tool, at the service of artists who are the true creators. We try to offer quality products, that's all we can do. We are servants of the world of art.

What is your favorite neighborhood in Paris?
Montparnasse is a neighborhood that we are fond of. It's a true Parisian quarter with quiet, little streets and a lot of artist studios. Giacometti took classes in sculpture on the rue de la Grande Chaumière [where Sennelier opened their second boutique in 1936 to cater to the many artists living and working in the neighborhood]. Historically it's so interesting, particularly during the Art Deco period and the roaring twenties.

A life-changing meeting?
There have been so many. But Henri Cartier-Bresson knew all four generations of our family. In the last twenty years of his life he focused on painting and drawing as his failing eyesight made photography difficult. He chose to work with egg tempera, which today is a little-known technique, but it was the first paint, before oil paint. And then Karl Lagerfeld knew three generations of the Senneliers. There was a certain ceremony around his visits, he came with his fan … but it was quite natural. He was charming and very kind. He bought lots of notebooks, lots of markers, lots of felt tips, lots of pens.

What is luxury?
Real privilege, true wealth, is culture. And we've had the chance to live in an environment where it is very present and so have been enriched by it a lot. Artists are people of great sensitivity and the world of art is a rich world, on all levels.

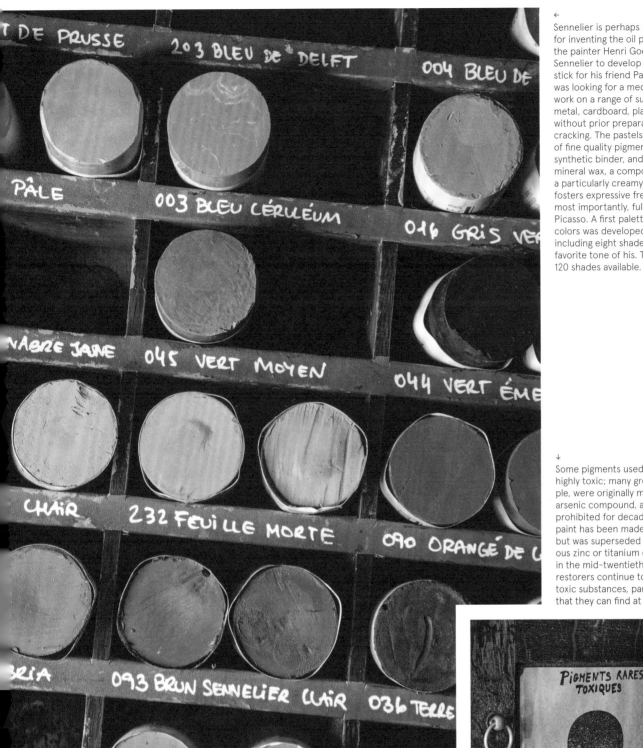

T DE PRUSSE   203 BLEU DE DELFT   004 BLEU DE

PÂLE   003 BLEU CÉRULÉUM   016 GRIS VER

NABRE JANE   045 VERT MOYEN   044 VERT ÉME

CHAIR   232 FEUILLE MORTE   090 ORANGÉ DE

BRIA   093 BRUN SENNELIER CLAIR   036 TERRE

Sennelier is perhaps most famous for inventing the oil pastel. In 1948, the painter Henri Goetz asked Henri Sennelier to develop a colored wax stick for his friend Pablo Picasso, who was looking for a medium that would work on a range of surfaces—wood, metal, cardboard, plastic, or paper—without prior preparation or fading or cracking. The pastels are composed of fine quality pigments, a very pure synthetic binder, and PH-neutral mineral wax, a composition with a particularly creamy texture that fosters expressive freedom, and, most importantly, fully satisfied Picasso. A first palette of forty-eight colors was developed for the artist, including eight shades of grey, a favorite tone of his. Today there are 120 shades available.

Some pigments used in the past were highly toxic; many greens, for example, were originally made from an arsenic compound, and have been prohibited for decades. Lead white paint has been made since antiquity but was superseded by less poisonous zinc or titanium compounds in the mid-twentieth century. Art restorers continue to use controlled toxic substances, particularly solvents that they can find at Sennelier.

PIGMENTS RARES TOXIQUES

+ BLOCKX + MICHAEL HARDING + WILLIAMSBURG

A detail from the color chart on display in the boutique that was hand-painted by Gustave Sennelier in 1926 illustrates the large palette of one hundred colors he offered for oil paints. We see the famous Hélios Red that was developed at the end of the twentieth century to provide artists with a more affordable alternative to Cadmium Red. The Chrome Yellows are no longer available however, as they brown in the sun, though Van Gogh loved their color and texture and used them often, most notably in his *Sunflowers* series.

Sophie & Dominique Sennelier

Magasin Sennelier
3 quai Voltaire, 75007 Paris
Saint-Germain-des-Prés,
METRO: Saint Germain des Prés
www.magasinsennelier.art

THE BOUTIQUE

"I think what works in this store is that we have kept it the same. It's not a copy of anything. It's not a supermarket. It's a true color merchant. And there's the idea of the dream. Artists need to dream; they need to explore very varied universes. It's a tiny little shop, but there are entire worlds inside." In addition to the products available for visual artists, the shop's shelves and drawers—dating back to 1860—contain many specialist products serving a range of crafts engaged in conservation and restoration, such as gilders, engravers, stone masons, book binders, or stained glass artisans, work that remains averse to industrial production. "The most beautiful things are things made by people. When a product is made by hand, it has something more sacred, more respectful, because we know there's a person behind it."

VINCENT FARRELLY & JEAN-BAPTISTE MARTIN

Domino papermakers, decorators
À Paris Chez Antoinette Poisson

In 2012 Vincent and Jean-Baptiste, trained paper conservators, were working on the restoration of an old house in the Auvergne region of France. Peeling back sheets of wallpaper, they discovered, seven layers in, the original decoration dating from the eighteenth century. Before printed rolls were invented, the first wallpapers, known as "domino papers," were rectangles of hand-colored, block-printed paper that were glued together then stuck on the wall. To restore the room to its original aspect, they decided to learn how to make and apply these domino papers themselves, following recently discovered technical drawings originally prepared for the famous eighteenth-century Enlightenment tome, *Encyclopédie*, edited by Denis Diderot and Jean le Rond d'Alembert.

The result was extraordinary. These experts in the life and times of the eighteenth century found themselves in a room that looked as it would have originally looked over two hundred years ago. The room shimmered with a certain beauty rare in the modern age—the special vibration of the handmade. Small variations in color and texture made for a unique energy and panache, and the duo immediately saw the technique's potential for contemporary interiors.

À Paris Chez Antoinette Poisson launched soon afterward, named after Louis XV's favorite mistress, Madame de Pompadour. "She was very keen on wallpaper, in fashion at the time because it was new." Born in 1721 as Antoinette Poisson, her life was contemporaneous with the relatively brief reign of domino papers, rendered obsolete by technological advances that made rolls and more complex printed finishes possible.

In their delightful shop in Paris, you can browse an ever-growing range of patterns available by the sheet, as roller wallpaper, notebooks, and a variety of retro items for the home, like a collection of dishes handmade out of papier-mâché or textiles such as cushions, plaids, and lampshades.

Some of Antoinette Poisson's motifs are copies of antique papers, and some are original creations, but all provide a bridge connecting us to the forgotten styles and atmospheres of the past, and might incite a small domestic revolution at your place.

↑
Domino papermakers in the eighteenth century printed with wooden blocks; À Paris chez Antoinette Poisson use metal plates, which are more stable and resilient. This pattern, No. 25 in their catalog, was inspired by the eighteenth-century papier-mâché box behind it, likely to have been originally used for hair powder, that Vincent and Jean-Baptiste picked up in an auction.

←
Vincent and Jean-Baptiste have documented every shade commonly used in eighteenth-century interiors in this reference book, making for a surprisingly bright palette. "Eighteenth-century houses were lit by candles, so bright colors on the walls reflected what light there was and imparted some freshness. We were surprised by how bright the oranges were. They loved color back then, inspired by textiles imported from India and China by the French East India Company."

↓
"When you look at our papers, you ask yourself is it an old one or not, you don't know really because the material is so close to an eighteenth-century paper." If the finished domino papers resemble those from the eighteenth century almost exactly, this is in part due to the rare papers they use. À Paris Chez Antoinette Poisson work with Le Moulin du Verger, an artisan paper mill dating back to the sixteenth century that revives pre-industrial papermaking techniques by using linen and hemp fibers rather than cellulose to make their papers.

Vincent Farrelly & Jean-Baptiste Martin

←
À Paris Chez Antoinette Poisson regularly work with other companies and designers like the Château de Versailles, Peter Marino, Ladurée, and Diptyque. Here a garment from Gucci's 2019 Cruise collection, developed around a collection of lavish custom patterns they designed in collaboration with creative director Alessandro Michele. The floor of Gucci's Wooster Street boutique in New York City was also decorated with an exclusive motif created by À Paris Chez Antoinette Poisson. "We are so proud of our recent collaborations with such important houses."

↓
The walls of the workshop and boutique are painted a shade of brown inspired by a color favored by Marie Antoinette which she named *caca-dauphin* ("dauphin poo") after a newborn prince's soiled diapers. "We were looking for a rather strong, unusual, and somewhat warm color." And if you're lucky, when you visit the store you might meet Pompon, the house mascot.

Describe your work.
Firstly, pattern designer, but also printer, painter, and decorator.

A life-changing meeting?
Just after setting up the company, we participated in the trade fair Maison & Objet in Paris for the first time; it was a challenge because it's expensive to rent a stand. On the first day, John Derian came by early in the morning and said, "I love that; I want that!" We were so happy, because it's such a great shop, such a great address in New York. He was really the first person to believe in us.

How do you explain your success?
I think we were in the right place at the right time. We don't use solvents, we don't use chemicals. Everything is natural and handmade, and at the moment there is a revival of craft and beautiful materials.

À Paris Chez Antoinette Poisson

↑
Decorative vintage chemistry bottles in the workshop. The team actually use high-quality modern inks that are lightfast, permanent, waterproof, and individually prepared for each new batch of domino papers.

→
In the eighteenth century, domino papers were not only used to decorate interiors, they were also common in the book trade, serving as paperback book bindings.

Vincent Farrelly & Jean-Baptiste Martin

VISIT

À Paris Chez Antoinette Poisson
12 rue Saint-Sabin, 75011 Paris
Bastille, METRO: Bréguet-Sabin
www.antoinettepoisson.com

REVOLUTIONARY ROOTS

À Paris Chez Antoinette Poisson have their studio and boutique on a pretty courtyard in the Bastille neighborhood that has been home to artisans for centuries. "As wallpaper manu-facturers, we have a special link with Bastille, specifically the Faubourg Saint-Antoine quarter. It was an important hub for wallpaper manufacturers in the eighteenth century. The biggest and most famous manufacturer was Réveillon, a royal manu-facturer, and the first violent outbreak of the French Revolution took place there; even before the taking of the Bastille, the royal wallpaper manufactory was ransacked and destroyed during a riot in 1789."

Vincent Farrelly & Jean-Baptiste Martin —

MATHIAS KISS

Artist-decorator
Mathias Kiss

From restoring the Louvre to features in *Wallpaper** magazine, the artist-decorator Mathias Kiss has traced the arc of his career through centuries of French decorative arts. After fifteen years as a painter-glazier for the Compagnons du Devoir, the extraordinary French craftsman's guild dating back to the Middle Ages, Mathias broke out of this highly codified system to explore new creative horizons.

Working with private collectors and commissions, as well as some of France's most emblematic luxury brands, Kiss reinvents and disrupts French decorative tropes—such as mirrors, moldings, frescoes, marble, gilt, and parquet—to create small- and large-scale installations that bridge the decorative arts with contemporary art.

Mathias and his team work out of two sites in Paris's historic Marais quarter: a tiny artisan's atelier—the back office—and a splendid showroom overlooking the Place des Vosges, a former seat of royalty built by Henry IV. Kiss's galleries are also located nearby. This triple Marais frontage plugs into different elements of the neighborhood's rich history: the French aristocracy and the grand homes they built there during the seventeenth and eighteenth centuries; the merchants and artisans, especially jewelers, goldsmiths, and silversmiths who moved into the increasingly popular area in the nineteenth century; and finally with the contemporary art galleries that arrived in the slipstream of the Musée Picasso from the mid-1980s.

The master painter and colorist who spent years perfecting, for example, trompe l'oeil frescoes depicting blue sky and clouds on the ceilings of nineteenth-century mansions, continues to take the sky as inspiration, but for horizontal panoramas or 3-D installations. He breaks mirrors out of their frames, brings moldings alive. Today, gold and silver leaves are less about wealth than minimalism, and his studies of marble are more hard rock than Second Empire.

→
A gilder cushion made of chamois leather, where the loose gold leaves are held. The parchment paper around the edge acts as a windshield.

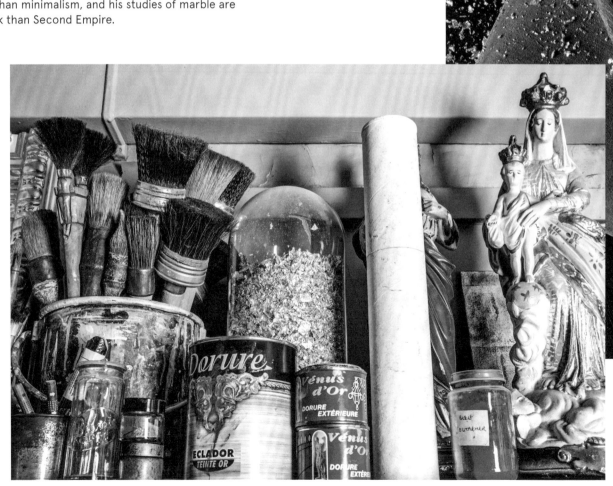

Mathias Kiss

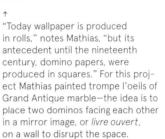

↑
"Today wallpaper is produced in rolls," notes Mathias, "but its antecedent until the nineteenth century, domino papers, were produced in squares." For this project Mathias painted trompe l'oeils of Grand Antique marble—the idea is to place two dominos facing each other in a mirror image, or *livre ouvert*, on a wall to disrupt the space.

↓
Preparatory models for the installation for *Wallpaper** magazine's *Handmade* show at the Salone del Mobile in Milan in 2013, for which Mathias Kiss collaborated with the historic Parisian wallpaper and fabric manufacturer Maison Pierre Frey.

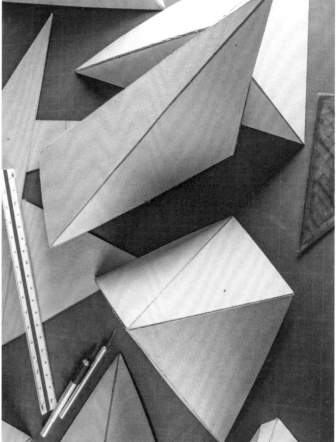

←
A painter and gilder's arsenal: brushes, jars, and tins of paint, lacquer, pigment, flakes of leftover gold leaf. *Bleu Outremer*—known as Ultramarine in English, and meaning in both English and French, "beyond the sea"—is a pigment originally made of ground lapis lazuli, which was once more expensive than gold. It was favored by Renaissance painters for the Virgin Mary's robes, for example. Since the nineteenth century a more vivid and affordable synthetic version exists.

Describe your work?
Let's say that I try to make things that belong to a story that I share with my clients.

What profession other than your own would you like to try?
I can't even imagine another profession as I don't believe I even have one. It's more that I'm just completely myself. Changing professions would be like changing heads.

What's a typical day for you?
A day where I get up and with sincerity go to the studio to push the engine forward, intellectually and physically. For me, the search for oneself happens through work.

Describe your studio?
A studio! A mess! A bit like my bedroom when I was a kid. There's toys all around.

Why do you work where you do?
The neighborhood, the light which is an absence of light, and my "cave," as I call it, is a decompression chamber that cuts me off from the world outside. It's wonderful!

What do you consider your greatest achievement?
The freedom to make, to say, to dream....

What is your favorite neighborhood in Paris?
The Marais forever! For the history that hits you in the face at every street corner. The absence of dreary avenues perpetuates the village that once was.

What is unique about Paris?
The assholes that live here. That is also the charm of Paris, to complain and frown without knowing why. So rare elsewhere....

Are you more "tradition" or "revolution"?
I'm tradition whose head I cut off.

Is there a secret to your job?
Yes.

↑
The large canvas facing the wall was a commission from Beyoncé for her album *4* and was returned to the studio after the shoot. "It's a sort of marble pattern; the brief was for something urban and energetic," explains Mathias. The blue-and-white marble motif on the back of the canvas was created for *Wallpaper** magazine's *Handmade* show at the Salone del Mobile in Milan in 2013. The pattern is inspired by Portor marble, which was particularly popular during the Second Empire. "When I was with the Compagnons, I was taken to see the Portor marble façade of the Cartier boutique on rue de la Paix to learn how to copy it in painting." Partially obscuring the marble motif is a photo from Mathias's old apartment capturing a trompe l'oeil of blue sky. As Mathias comments, "There's always an aspect of illusion and escape to my work." The gold punching bag in the corner was commissioned by a collector and Mathias, a former professional Thai boxer, made a second one for himself. "A punching bag is normally something rough, maltreated, covered with sweat; the complete opposite to the precious finish it has here."

VISIT

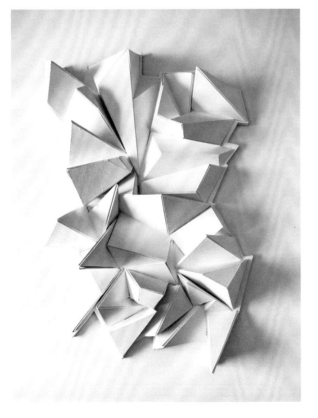

Mathias Kiss Showroom
2 rue des Francs-Bourgeois,
75003 Paris
Marais, METRO: Rambuteau
Open by appointment only
www.mathiaskiss.com

BESTSELLER

A cardboard maquette of the three-dimensional mirror, *Miroir Froissé, Sans 90°* ("*No Right Angle*"). "My hit! Coming from the Compagnons du Devoir, with their symbol, like the Masons, of the square and the compass, where measurements are so important, to call it 'No Right Angle' is quite significant. With this piece I wanted to break with my masters. I entered the craftsman's guild at fourteen, and they not only educated me, they raised me. For fifteen years or more I was constantly reprimanded: it must be straight, a molding must mark the perimeter of a room, it must be closed, etc. So this piece marks a real rupture."

PIERRE HARDY

Shoe designer
Pierre Hardy

Designer since 1990 of the shoe collections of France's oldest and most emblematic luxury label, Hermès, and since 2001 of its jewelry collections too, Pierre Hardy launched his own accessories label in 1999. If not a household name, he's a favorite with the "thinking" fashion set. Pierre Hardy shoes are elegant architectural constructions that play with geometric volume, bold patterns, and color.

Behind Pierre Hardy's desk hangs a framed original by genius fashion photographer Guy Bourdin that makes visible the Parisian designer's first (fashion) fantasy. Shot for a Charles Jourdan campaign from Spring 1978, a woman in a tight red dress with matching heels stands on a ladder whose ends are out of frame in front of a wall of white shoeboxes—she's on an endless quest inside a giant shoe shop. This dreamscape was burned into Hardy's imagination as a young man, setting the scene for his creative destiny.

Hardy leads an elegant and idiosyncratic career that seems propelled as much by pleasure, inspiration, and lucky encounters as by ambition. Studies at the prestigious École normale supérieure should have led Hardy to a career teaching theater design, but his understanding of how to stage and dramatize objects and people took him on a different journey. His passion for modern dance added insight into constraining and transforming the body, as well as perhaps the erotic potential of ankles and arches. Fine drawing skills gave him the ability to get it all down on paper with style to spare.

If he's usually associated with a certain idea of the avantgarde, Hardy is a self-proclaimed classicist, with an aesthetic matrix he claims is born out of the vistas and atmospheres of Paris's old streets, stones, and salons. His designs articulate classical proportions, restraint, and symmetry but with a contemporary vocabulary. His flagship is a tête-à-tête with the past too. A monochrome black (shoe) box, it's located under the exquisite arcades of the Palais-Royal, the former eighteenth-century palace and garden hidden behind the Louvre. A place as beautiful and discreet as his label.

↑
A wooden ladder leans against the wall in a corner of Pierre's office with a magazine clipped open to a spread by Helmut Newton from the 1970s. A recurring motif, the ladder has served as a mode of display since the first Pierre Hardy collection when he hooked shoes over the rungs by their heels. Pierre was originally inspired by a Warhol illustration commissioned by *Glamour* magazine in the 1950s. Perhaps more than fashion references, he is inspired by art and artists including Donald Judd, Ellsworth Kelly, and Sol LeWitt.

↑
"My collections are not the illustration of a story. I do not write a scenario and then create the shoes for the characters. I work more on the shapes, the colors, the composition. It's funny, even if at first the idea was rather Ellsworth Kelly, in the end this collection tells a much more fanciful, much lighter, much more Italian, and much more feminine story. But I think that's also the story of fashion. In the end the idea is still to make objects that are sensual, that dress women, that create desire."

Pierre Hardy

→
Hardy's drawing tools: pencil lead refill, a circle template, a brass Midori ruler, a Bluetooth stylus, a Mono Zero eraser, a Mont Blanc pen, and a Mont Blanc mechanical pencil. Hardy designs using pencil and paper, but loves working on tablet and iPhone too, using, for example, the Brushes Redux app to create the "seasonal images" that illustrate the essence of each new collection. He also goes digital in the back-and-forth with his design and manufacturing teams, making adjustments directly onto photos exchanged by email.

↓
Rolls of leather from past collections in the design studio include a couple variations of the house's "Cube Perspective" monogrammed canvas introduced in 2010. Though generally not a fan of pattern, Pierre has long found the trompe l'oeil motif inspiring in its graphic geometry. The now iconic print is reimagined for each collection to reflect the season's color palette.

Pierre Hardy

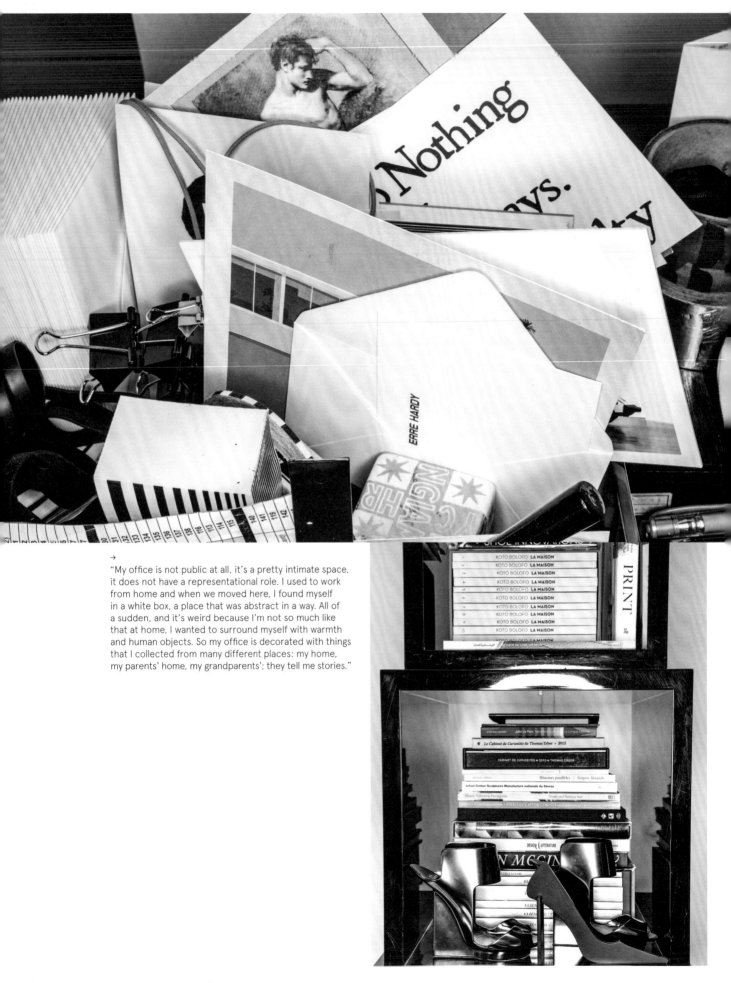

→
"My office is not public at all, it's a pretty intimate space, it does not have a representational role. I used to work from home and when we moved here, I found myself in a white box, a place that was abstract in a way. All of a sudden, and it's weird because I'm not so much like that at home, I wanted to surround myself with warmth and human objects. So my office is decorated with things that I collected from many different places: my home, my parents' home, my grandparents'; they tell me stories."

What's a typical day for you?
The reason I've been doing my job for so long is because no two days are ever the same. The concepts can be similar, but the way you go about them makes each day different from the last. I feel very lucky.

What is your favorite tool?
I only need a paper and a pencil. Drawing for me is the quickest, easiest, and most genuine way to start designing a collection. It allows me to visualize the collection and also serves as a way to verify if an idea actually works. I draw everywhere. A bit like a smoker, you see, who turns everything into an ashtray.

What inspires you?
I find inspiration everywhere! It could be anything from colors to museums to a landscape. It's a chemistry. I cannot explain when, why, or what. It's like falling in love with someone. You can analyze it in a way, but you have no idea when it will hit.

What is luxury?
I think that many notions have been grafted on to it that are more to do with service, efficiency, speed, customization … a whole lot of stuff that's been piled on top of simply rarity, or the perfectly made, which for me are closer to a true definition of luxury than any marketing or merchandising.

What is your favorite neighborhood in Paris?
I think the Palais-Royal is the most beautiful place in Paris. It mixes paradoxical qualities: it's in the center but a little hidden; it's very open but at the same time it's enclosed; it's inside, it's outside. I love the promenade under the arcades, where you can walk in any weather: you're in the shade in summer, sheltered when it rains. I love that.

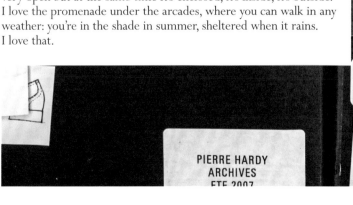

VISIT

Pierre Hardy
156 galerie de Valois,
Jardin du Palais Royal, 75001 Paris
Palais-Royal, METRO: Palais Royal–
Musée du Louvre
www.pierrehardy.com

THE LOCATION

Pierre Hardy's first boutique opened in 2003 under the arcades of the Palais-Royal. A monochrome black box, it channels the house's minimal, radical, and graphic attitude, setting up an invigorating interplay with its surroundings. The different vocabularies of the Palais-Royal's classic architecture and gardens, the artist Daniel Buren's iconic striped columns installed in the *cour d'honneur* nearby, and the Pierre Hardy space and collections all intermingle to produce a uniquely Parisian vibe.

ALAIN DUCASSE

Chef, entrepreneur
Le Chocolat Alain Ducasse

Le Chocolat Alain Ducasse

Hidden in the Bastille quarter's warren of streets is Paris's only bean-to-bar chocolate factory, La Manufacture de Chocolat Alain Ducasse. Here, in a former Renault garage, the famous French chef's expert team toils over a range of unique chocolates: pralines prepared with almonds, hazelnuts, pistachios, peanuts, or roasted coconut; truffles dusted in cocoa and flavored with orange; ganaches dedicated to the aroma of a single terroir or flavored with ingredients such as fresh mint, Earl Grey tea and lemon, coffee, caramel, passionfruit, or lime. The Manufacture sells a relatively short range of products, the idea is to go deeper rather than wider.

Operating on a rare, artisanal scale, it is the only chocolate manufactory in Paris to master the entire process, starting with sourcing the beans. Most chocolate makers buy their chocolate—of exceptional quality perhaps—ready-made from an industrial manufacturer, with a texture and flavor that are already defined. The idea behind this chocolate factory is to know the origin of each cocoa bean, who grows it, and to follow the entire manufacturing process down to the finished product. Ducasse and his team are constantly looking to perfect the sourcing of the raw materials—of the beans of course, but also the quality of the sugar, of the powdered milk, and of all the ingredients used to fill and flavor the chocolate.

Alain Ducasse has spent his career striving for perfection, always working to be "faster and better!" His exceptional drive is often explained by his fabled brush with death in 1984, the only survivor of a light plane crash in the Alps. Today he is at the head of a global empire of thirty-one restaurants throughout seven countries. His tables can be found inside some of Paris's most famous monuments and palace hotels, from the Louvre to the Hôtel Plaza Athénée. At the Château de Versailles, he even works with the gardeners to grow vegetables that will be served in his restaurants. On the Seine, a custom-made electric boat takes foodies on a sightseeing epicurean cruise.

Chef, businessman, and brand, Alain Ducasse has founded his success on a lifelong respect for authenticity and produce; in whatever he does he is always striving to bring out the natural identity of fine ingredients. He's also an ace at bringing out the best in his many collaborators. His chocolate project was originally developed with his longstanding collaborator, the pastry chef Nicolas Berger. Both Ducasse and Berger, who is originally from Lyon, were inspired by historic Lyon chocolatier Maurice Bernachon. Their dream and unstinting effort means that today, for just a handful of euros, lucky customers have the chance to enjoy one of life's little luxuries: a chocolate bonbon prepared with the best in quality, expertise, time, and care.

↑
Three stages are critical for the taste of the chocolate: the selection of the beans, the roasting, and conching. This old Virey-Garnier roaster was previously used for coffee so it had to have its temperature and speed adjusted for roasting cocoa beans. "We maintain a constant temperature to roast cocoa beans; it's actually about drying the bean well."

←
The unique flavor of a chocolate depends on its origin. The beans for Ducasse chocolate are sourced from about a dozen different origins—Madagascar, Venezuela, Java, Trinidad, India, Nicaragua—each with its own identity and aroma. Cocoa pods are harvested twice a year. After the pods are split open with a machete, the beans are sorted and then placed in wooden crates to ferment for three to six days before being dried in the sun, then packed in 150 pound (70 kg) bags for shipping.

→
After roasting, the beans go through a winnowing machine, a *casse-cacao* where they are cracked and the husks are removed, leaving only the crushed nibs. This vintage Carle & Montanari machine was recovered in an old Italian factory and reassembled by a craftsman in Paris. It "processes roughly two hundred kilos per hour; if I wanted a machine that processed two tons per hour I could have found it easily."

Are you more tradition or revolution?

I prefer the word innovation. Chocolate opens doors to imagination and creation. It demands a high level of method, precision, and proficiency.

What is unique about your work?

For over thirty years, my fascination with chocolate never left me and took true form with the opening of the Manufacture in 2013. My philosophy has always been based on a rigorous selection of quality raw materials, fully exposing their original flavors and fragrances. I am proud of our team—we make the chocolate from start to finish, beginning with selecting the very best beans from around the world.

What inspires you?

The desire to always be different, ahead of the pack, and at the best quality. And to share this ambition with every member of the team.

What is your favorite neighborhood in Paris and why?

Bastille, where La Manufacture is located. I can't resist drawing a parallel between the Revolution, which started here, and our revolutionary approach to chocolate.

← Alain Ducasse chocolates are sold in simple brown paper packets or cardboard boxes with metallic embossing, which brings a precious, delicate aspect to the ensemble. "Sometimes we've had an idea for a product, but in the end, the packaging would have become too complicated, so we abandon the idea. There's no point in just selling packaging."

VISIT

La Manufacture de Chocolat Alain Ducasse
40 rue de la Roquette, 75011 Paris
Bastille, METRO: Bastille
www.lechocolat-alainducasse.com

THE BOUTIQUE

The shop is connected to the factory, with only windows in between, so all the action in the factory is visible in the shop too, which is fragrant with all the amazing smells! "Today when you enter a chocolate shop, there is often no odor as the shop must be a little cool to preserve the chocolate. I didn't want that!" Both spaces are decorated using the same simple materials, the same concrete floor, the same black steel. Alain Ducasse found most of the vintage furniture and fittings at the Saint-Ouen Flea Market. The chocolates are displayed in furniture originating from the Bank of France in Amiens, and the suspension lamps were originally installed in a 1930s navy boat.

APOLLONIA POILÂNE

Baker
Poilâne

When Apollonia Poilâne was studying at Harvard, she had
a loaf of Poilâne sourdough FedExed to her every week for
four years. It wasn't just homesickness: "That slice of bread
and butter nourished me, provided the sufficient fuel to get
through the morning. On mornings when I had no Poilâne
bread I was miserable."

While getting her economics degree in the US, Apollonia was
also running the family business of 160 employees back in Paris.
She had taken the reins at just eighteen years old after her
parents died in a helicopter accident in 2002.

The Poilâne saga began seventy years prior, in 1932, when
her paternal grandfather Pierre moved to Paris from Normandy
with his Swiss wife and set up a bakery in bohemian Saint-
Germain-des-Prés. Rather than the more chic baguette made
with refined white flour, they chose instead to specialize in big
loaves of a nutritious country-style sourdough bread made
with stone-ground flour rich in wheatgerm.

→
The famous Poilâne sourdough loaves
fresh out of the oven. The traditional
breadmaking techniques used by Poilâne
result in the sourdough loaf's signature
thick and floury crust. Contact with the
heat in the wood-fired oven caramel-
izes the starches in the dough, turning
the loaf brown and crunchy, which you
won't find on bread cooked in an electric oven. Apollonia recommends melting leftover cheese in a pan with cumin
seeds and eating it served over toasted
crusts, a Poilâne family tradition on
Sunday nights.

↑

Except for Sundays, Poilâne's bread, biscuits, and baker's pastries are prepared here in the basement of the historic boutique, which has been operating as a bakery since 1791. The bakery operates twenty-four hours a day, six days a week, producing forty to fifty loaves a batch from the oven.
Each loaf takes six hours to make. Using traditional methods, a piece of dough from one batch
serves as a starter for the next. The dough is kneaded in a kneading machine, followed by slow
fermentation, shaping, and proofing, before being scored with a letter P and baked for one hour
in the wood-fired brick oven. "What is really unique and special is the fact they that we are able to
have such consistency in the quality of our products because of our bakers' expertise."

Apollonia Poilâne

149

Thirty years later, Apollonia's father, Lionel, opened new bakeries in Paris and London and set up an innovative "manu-factory" just outside Paris that allowed Poilâne to supply thousands of retail outlets while maintaining the house's traditional fabrication techniques—what he called "retro-innovation"—which really put the house on the map internationally. Lionel also showed great marketing savvy by fostering celebrity clients like Frank Sinatra, Lauren Bacall, and Robert De Niro, as well as artistic collaborations, most famously with Salvador Dalí.

If today Poilâne bakers use a machine rather than their bare hands to knead the dough, not much else has changed since 1932. The Poilâne sourdough is still prepared in the basement of the rue du Cherche-Midi bakery from starter, stone-ground flour, Guérande sea salt, and water, then baked in the ancient wood-fired oven there. The baker's craft remains unchanged—transforming, via fermentation and cooking, flour, salt, and water into a rich and complex product. Today Apollonia sees much of her role as guaranteeing the quality of these raw materials, working hand in hand with flour millers and salt producers that have sometimes collaborated with the bakery for generations, to produce truly nourishing and flavorsome bread.

↑
Apollonia's father Lionel famously struck up a friendship with Salvador Dalí in the 1960s. Dalí commissioned a series of Surrealist objects from the baker, beginning with a bird-cage made out of bread—so the bird could peck its way to freedom!—and finally an entire set of bedroom furniture, as Dalí wanted to see if he had mice in his suite in the Meurice. The bread chandelier in the shop's backroom is a nod to this collaboration and is remade every two years or so. "It's more or less always the same, but this version has little birds on it."

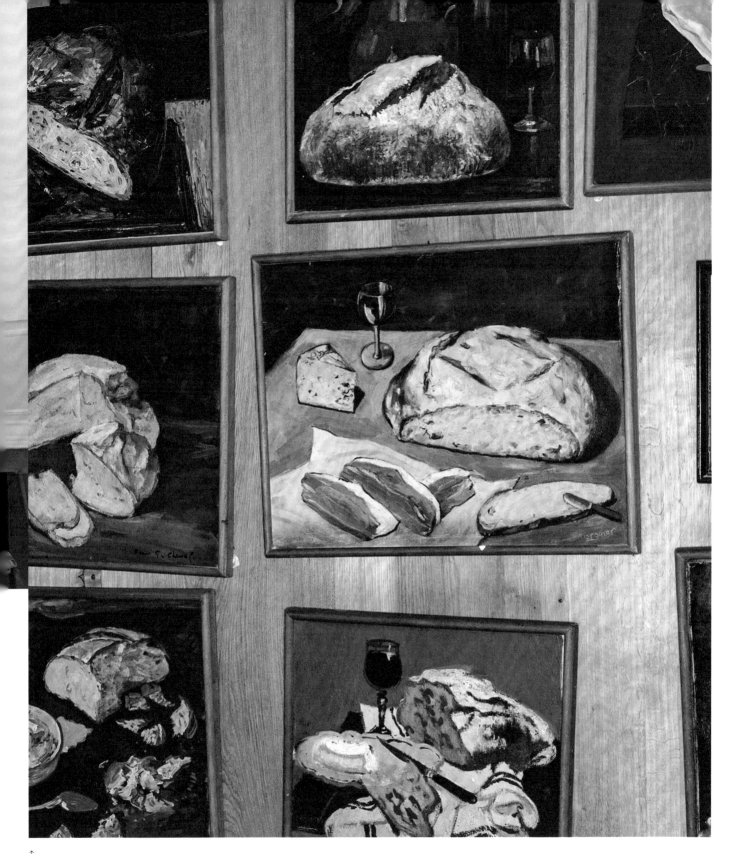

↑
The wood-paneled backroom behind the shop at rue du Cherche-Midi is at the heart of the bakery's daily operations, and a genuine artifact of Parisian and Saint-Germain-des-Prés history. The walls are covered with many paintings, predominantly still lifes with bread, hung salon-style. When Pierre Poilâne arrived here in the early 1930s, "the neighborhood was filled with artists who couldn't quite pay for their bread, so they bartered bread for paintings." The little room acts as a buffer between the public space of the shop and the production areas behind and downstairs. Like her father before her, Apollonia uses the space as her office.

Describe your profession.
To transform cereals into bread by the process of fermentation.
To make bread that nourishes and lasts.

Is there a secret to your job?
Passion, the application of the five senses, time.

Why do you work where you do?
Poilâne is my family's business. So it's atavistic, but there's also
a sincere love for my profession, for its simplicity and richness.

What is unique about your work?
Each batch is unique, each loaf is unique because it's made by hand
and because bread is a living product.

Describe your atelier.
The bakehouse is a kind of nourishing cocoon. The heat envelopes,
the perfumes intoxicate, the light caresses, and the sounds of the
shop above anchor this timeless and otherworldly place.

What is unique about Paris?
Paris is a compendium of quarters with very different personalities, but with such proximity that you can easily navigate between
worlds that are more naturally in opposition.

What is your favorite neighborhood in Paris?
I have a soft spot for Saint-Germain-des-Prés. Memories of my
parents; what I'm building here with my friends; the neighborhood's new traditions … just as many seeds for new chapters and
experiences in this quarter, with its multiple facets and stories.

Are you more "tradition" or "revolution"?
More "retro-innovation": the best of both worlds!

↑
This ancient Roman scale is still used to confirm the weight of each loaf that passes through the baker's hands. "Baking is above all a sensory experience: you're always adapting to your environment, baking to that day's specific conditions, so for me it's about your eyesight of course, and your hands that are able to touch the dough and feel how it's stretching that day, how it's reacting to the shaping of the loaves and so forth."

Poilâne
8 rue du Cherche-Midi,
75006 Paris
Saint-Germain-des-Prés,
METRO: Saint-Sulpice
www.poilane.com

BEYOND BREAD

As well as bread, the bakery makes biscuits and baker's pastries or *viennoiseries* (pastries that can be baked in a bread oven), including croissants, *pains au chocolat* and apple and custard tarts. Here we see the house's famous short-breads called *punitions* ("punishments"). In tune with her vision and the times, Apollonia has added rye and buckwheat versions to the menu. The bakery also sells a small range of complementary products, from delicious jams or the perfect bread knife to the best Japanese soba tea. And next door at their café, Comptoir Poilâne, you can enjoy one of their open-faced sandwiches prepared with Poilâne bread, or perhaps a croissant fresh out of the oven and dunked in a hot bowl of café au lait.

Apollonia Poilâne —

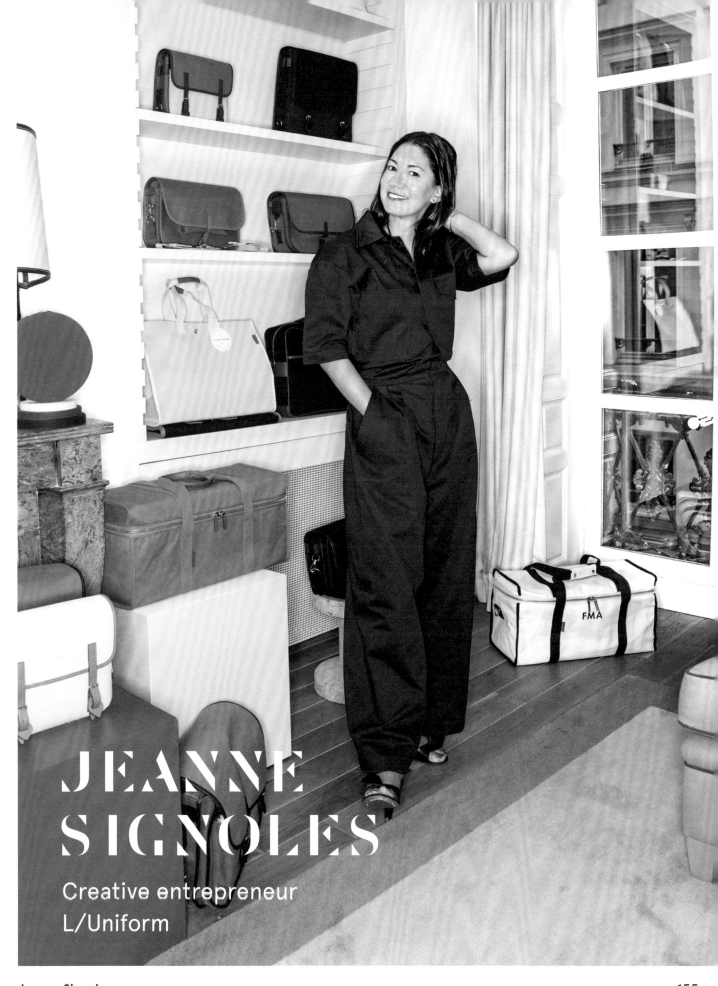

JEANNE SIGNOLES

Creative entrepreneur
L/Uniform

The knapsack, the shopping tote, the satchel, the backpack, the tool bag, the duffle bag, the vanity. L/Uniform resurrects bag archetypes as reasonably priced utilitarian items that are unisex and timeless and perfectly adapted to modern life. All L/Uniform bags are crafted out of quality woven canvas; trims and handles come in leather or sturdy cotton grosgrain; bag hardware and logo are discreet and unfussy. For all that, a L/Uniform bag has unique style—elegant and playful—owing to perfect proportions and inspired color palettes. Each bag provides boundless possibilities for bag and trim color combinations.

Jeanne Signoles and her husband Alex set up L/Uniform in 2013 with the idea to bring "beauty to the useful." Before this, Jeanne worked for the family business, the heritage Parisian trunk maker Goyard, which her father-in-law bought from the Goyard family twenty years ago. If Goyard seduces the likes of Meghan Markle or Pharrell Williams by selling exclusively via a handful of dedicated *comptoirs*, L/Uniform launched with an international e-shop and aims for something digital and democratic. "We're not a fashion brand, we're an everyday brand." What the two companies have in common are dedicated ateliers in Carcassonne, and also in Portugal for L/Uniform and an exquisite attention to quality workmanship and materials. "We have our own workshops. Which is the thing that makes the difference. Every week, I see the development teams, we discuss current projects and I share my aspirations with them. In general, I take a model of bag—because I don't invent anything—or I explain with words, or materials, or colors."

Born and raised in Bordeaux, Jeanne moved to Toulouse for her studies. After completing a master's degree in econometrics she joined aerospace giant Airbus before coming to Paris to work in investment banking. She sees her mathematically trained mind as being crucial to the success of her house, and though she is modest about her creative input in the bag designs, she thoroughly owns up to the innovative vision behind the successful brand. "It's the most interesting part, to build a history, an identity, to have a logical DNA, to show that all these ideas are connected by a thread, which means that they are all logical. That's mathematics, and that's really interesting. And the more you explain your story, the more logical it becomes, the more you can make it fluid, and the more you believe in it."

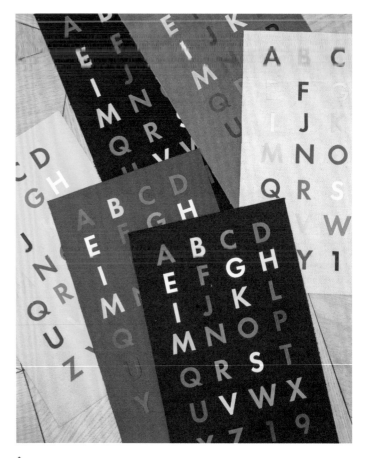

↑
Every L/Uniform bag can be silkscreened with a personal monogram up to three characters long in a choice of eight colors "to really make a uniform that's yours and not someone else's ... it can be your initials, it can be a number too, it can even just be a single letter. There's a girl, she just wants an 'S.'"

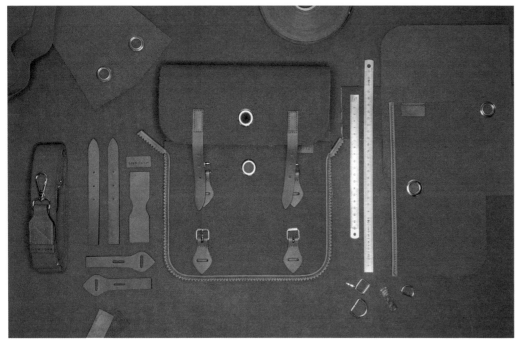

←
A deconstructed view of L/Uniform's very first design, modeled after the classic US Army satchel. "I invent nothing. Our satchel is a US Army satchel. I adapted it a little, to a particular scale, but otherwise it's exactly the same. It's with the choice of materials and colors that I contribute something."

→
In true utilitarian style, each packet is stamped after purchase with the bag's unique identity number.

N°43

L/
UNI
FORM

MANUFACTURE · CARCASSONNE ·

↑
Every bag purchased in the shop can be customized immediately with the on-site monogram machine.

←
The Cooler Bag No. 95 is lined with isothermal fabric to keep your snacks cool.

→
Jeanne holds her 1950s style, Carry On Suitcase No. 40 in red, mono-grammed with her initials in navy blue and with brown leather piping around the edges. "We have a special order service. You pay the same price, but you have the possibility to choose the color of the canvas and the trim-mings, the monogram. This makes for an infinite number of combinations. It's not more expensive, it's just that you have to wait a little. The idea also is not to stock ten billion different pieces at the factory."

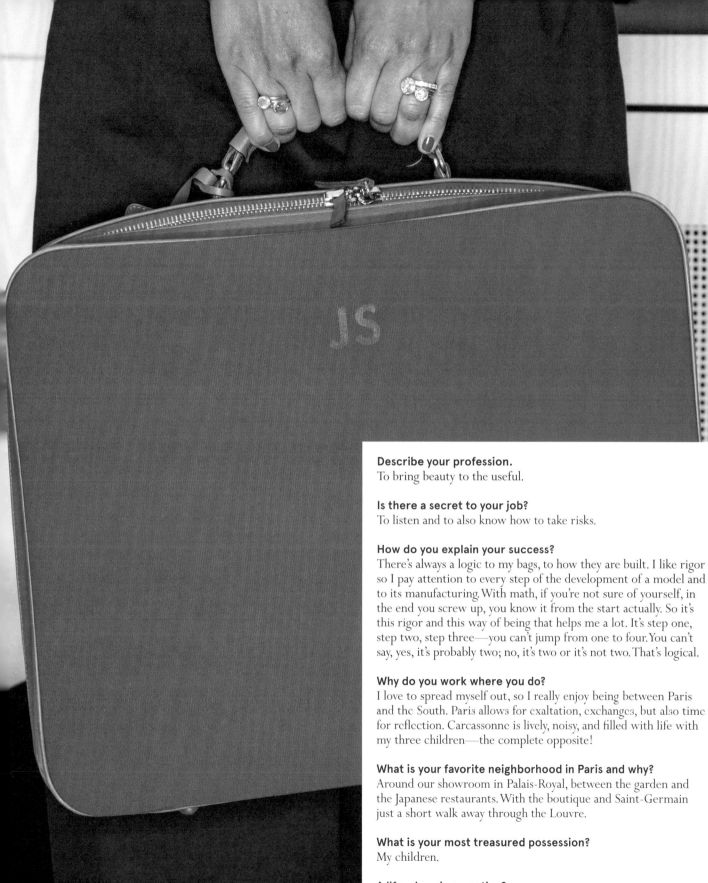

Describe your profession.
To bring beauty to the useful.

Is there a secret to your job?
To listen and to also know how to take risks.

How do you explain your success?
There's always a logic to my bags, to how they are built. I like rigor so I pay attention to every step of the development of a model and to its manufacturing. With math, if you're not sure of yourself, in the end you screw up, you know it from the start actually. So it's this rigor and this way of being that helps me a lot. It's step one, step two, step three—you can't jump from one to four. You can't say, yes, it's probably two; no, it's two or it's not two. That's logical.

Why do you work where you do?
I love to spread myself out, so I really enjoy being between Paris and the South. Paris allows for exaltation, exchanges, but also time for reflection. Carcassonne is lively, noisy, and filled with life with my three children—the complete opposite!

What is your favorite neighborhood in Paris and why?
Around our showroom in Palais-Royal, between the garden and the Japanese restaurants. With the boutique and Saint-Germain just a short walk away through the Louvre.

What is your most treasured possession?
My children.

A life-changing meeting?
My husband.

What is your greatest extravagance?
I'm not extravagant.

THE BOUTIQUE

L/Uniform has a little shop on the Left Bank of the Seine, overlooking the Louvre. Masamichi Katayama of forward-thinking Tokyo interior design firm Wonderwall designed the long, narrow space to feel like a futuristic cabinet of curiosities. The different bag models are displayed in custom boxes piled up to the ceiling like tiny wonder windows. A digital screen flashes with still lifes, short films, or images of bags interspersed with accessory-inspired quotes from popular culture like James Brown's "Papa's got a brand new bag." In the back, a change of scenery with a sort of diorama of a workshop, where the various tools and materials used to make each L/Uniform bag are displayed on wooden walls, allowing customers to visualize materials and finishes. In 2019, L/Uniform opened a second store in the Marunouchi quarter of Tokyo, also designed by Wonderwall.

VISIT

L/Uniform
21 Quai Malaquais, 75006 Paris
Saint-Germain-des-Prés,
METRO: Saint-Germain-des-Prés
www.luniform.com

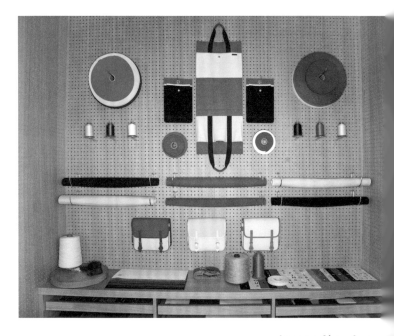

Jeanne Signoles —

VICTOIRE DE TAILLAC-TOUHAMI & RAMDANE TOUHAMI

Creative entrepreneurs
L'Officine Universelle Buly

Natural beauty brand L'Officine Universelle Buly, Buly for short, was partly inspired by the title character of the nineteenth-century Balzac novel César Birotteau, who in turn was based on the real-life Parisian perfumer Jean-Vincent Bully, famous for his "vinaigre de toilette" skin tonic and other cosmetic innovations before he went broke. But Buly is hardly a literal reboot of a vintage brand; it's more a pretext for Victoire and Ramdane's very playful, very detailed, and very personal fantasy: a potpourri of everything they like—the mythology of Paris, a Japanese attention to detail, state-of-the-art natural cosmetics, and ancestral beauty remedies—and what they're good at, namely resonant storytelling and ingenious staging.

The background to this larger-than-life husband-and-wife team is as rich and fanciful as their brand. In short, the bad-boy son of Moroccan immigrants launches a skater-inspired T-shirt brand called Teuchiland in his hometown of Montauban; gets some notoriety which attracts the attention of a local gang; he flees to Paris in 1996 where he lives on the streets and almost dies after getting stabbed in the leg; then in 1997 he cofounds a short-lived but headline-grabbing Marais concept store called L'Épicerie, before meeting Parisian public relations executive and high society girl ... you can Google for complete details.

Since Victoire and Ramdane met in 1999, they have been working as an entrepreneurial tag team—a kind of creative good cop/bad cop duo where "Ramdane has the ideas, I see how to knit them together," explains Victoire. Their first collaboration in 2001 was the innovative Parisian beauty bar Parfumerie Générale. Then in 2006 they relaunched French heritage candlemaker Cire Trudon, founded in 1643. Ramdane turned the slumbering former royal wax manufacturer's fortunes around, introducing scented candles with Proustian aromas, such as the Solis Rex, "inspired by the elaborate parquetry of Château de Versailles's famous Hall of Mirrors," and *boules puantes* (perfumed stink bombs), before selling his shares in 2011.

In 2014 Buly was born and today two Officines in Paris act as dreamy portals connecting the dots between Ramdane's hyperactive imagination and ambition, Victoire's aristocratic culture and her natural beauty expertise, and their sumptuous improvisation on Paris, in which the city's refinement and history collide with contemporary craftsmanship and beauty.

↑
Buly resists the digital age with a unique calligraphy service. All staff take weekly classes while in-house c rapher Bruno is on hand to customize purchases or write telegrams or other elegant notes on your beha Important clients receive a personal handwritten me on their birthdays in the mail.

ORIGINE	NUMÉRO	NOMBRE DE MOTS	DATE DE DÉPÔT	HEURE DE DÉPÔT	MENTION DE SERVICE

Dear Ginger,

he Officine is pleased to wish you a very hap Birthday.

are happy to count you among our Customers

See You Soon,

Officine Universelle Buly

● Pour toute réclamation concernant ce télégramme, présenter cette formule au bureau distributeur. ●
326. o. VOIR AU VERSO la signification des principales indications qui peuvent éventuellement figurer en tête

→
Plant oils have been important for Buly since the beginning. Extracted from a variety of grains, fruits, flowers, and roots, the oils can be used to hydrate and nourish the body, face, hair, and nails. Today the brand offers 120 kinds, so there's something for absolutely everyone. Victoire's favorite is the Huile Antique, a natural scented dry body oil: "used in the morning it gives you energy and lifts your mood."

Victoire de Taillac-Touhami & Ramdane Touhami

↑
Much research goes into developing Buly's huge selection of over seven hundred different products. They revive an infinitude of beauty rituals with fascinating, sometimes obscure cosmetics and accessories sourced from traditions from all around the world: volcanic pumice stones from Italy, antiperspirant alum stone, natural sea sponges from Greece, and Ayurvedic vetiver root exfoliating pads. They also offer all sorts of brushes and combs such as Japanese Suvé body brushes, toothbrushes made with silk or badger bristles, and acetate combs from Switzerland. "Part of why we love Buly is that it's endless," explains Victoire.

↑
Ramdane and Victoire's office at the back of the rue de Saintonge store. In the corner an antique perfume distiller has been transformed into a lamp; in the foreground, a mini recording studio for podcasts; an antique brass clothes rack stands in front of a world map commissioned from a Japanese illustrator in the style of embroidered Sukajan jackets. The pictures on the wall are original posters from the May 1968 uprisings in Paris: "Capitulation doesn't pay!"

→ "I don't work much at my desk;
I put things on it. I rarely sit down,"
says Ramdane.

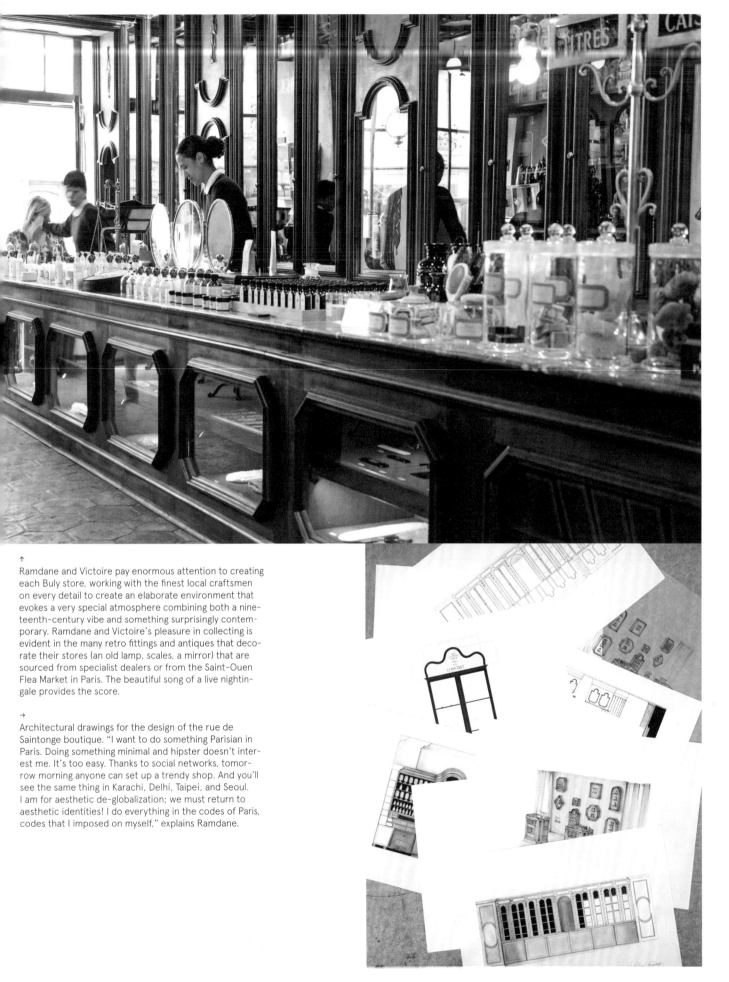

↑
Ramdane and Victoire pay enormous attention to creating each Buly store, working with the finest local craftsmen on every detail to create an elaborate environment that evokes a very special atmosphere combining both a nineteenth-century vibe and something surprisingly contemporary. Ramdane and Victoire's pleasure in collecting is evident in the many retro fittings and antiques that decorate their stores (an old lamp, scales, a mirror) that are sourced from specialist dealers or from the Saint-Ouen Flea Market in Paris. The beautiful song of a live nightingale provides the score.

→
Architectural drawings for the design of the rue de Saintonge boutique. "I want to do something Parisian in Paris. Doing something minimal and hipster doesn't interest me. It's too easy. Thanks to social networks, tomorrow morning anyone can set up a trendy shop. And you'll see the same thing in Karachi, Delhi, Taipei, and Seoul. I am for aesthetic de-globalization; we must return to aesthetic identities! I do everything in the codes of Paris, codes that I imposed on myself," explains Ramdane.

What is unique about your work?
V: Buly is a very personal project, a mix of everything that we like. There's no logic. It's not literal. It's a complete fantasy; a fantasy of the ideal, traditional perfume store, but really it's our fantasy of Paris.

Describe your profession.
R: I am not a serial entrepreneur. I don't give a damn about being a serial entrepreneur. I am a guy who has ideas and wants to make them happen. So I invent. Because other people don't give me work, I make up my own stuff.

What inspires you?
V: The Japanese are a big influence because of their dedication to detail; it's such a beautiful country for creative retail and for service.

What do you consider your greatest achievement?
R: That you start with an idea, a blank sheet of paper, and four years later you have 250 people who live from it.

Is there a secret to your job?
R: I am fascinated by managers, people who manage humans. Because in our business this is the hardest part. I can create a new product in fifteen minutes but it's very complicated to motivate people for the same project, to make it competitive and successful.

What is unique about Paris?
R: I like its disgruntled side; I hate when I go to a city where everyone's nice.

What is luxury?
R: This feeling of being unique, of having something only for oneself, that's what's rotten. In the world we live in; what stupidity! We are supposed to be saving the planet!

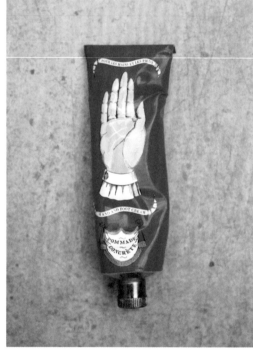

L'Officine Universelle Buly
www.buly1803.com

45 rue de Saintonge, 75003 Paris
Northern Marais, METRO: Filles du Calvaire

6 rue Bonaparte, 75006 Paris
Saint-Germain-des-Prés,
METRO: Saint-Germain-des-Prés

BESTSELLER

The *Pommade Concrète* hand and foot cream
was one of the first products Ramdane developed for Buly; nourishing and fragrance-free,
it has been a bestseller since day one. Buly
uses no plastics for their packaging, so the
Pommade Concrète comes in a metal tube,
while other products are sold in glass, ceramic,
or paper. If Buly's packaging screams nineteenth-century chic, the formulations are
totally twenty-first century: free of para-
bens, phenoxyethanol, and silicone, and soon
to all be certified organic too. Buly products are made in France in Cosmetic Valley,
an innovative technopole dedicated to the
perfume and cosmetics industries founded in
1994 on the initiative of Jean-Paul Guerlain,
the fourth-generation *parfumeur* of the
legendary house.

Victoire de Taillac-Touhami & Ramdane Touhami —

MARIE & ALEXANDRE THUMERELLE

Booksellers, publishers
Ofr.

Ofr. is an independent arts bookshop, gallery, and publisher in Paris.... Let's start again! Ofr. is a bohemian utopia, a creative forcehold, a machine for ideas, a drop-in center for the city's artists, punks, and dreamers. On any day of the week, pass by, get inspired, see what happens. Bring your kids. Browse the books on the tables out front, sit on one of the benches and enjoy the sunshine, or meet a new friend. Wander inside, lose yourself in the selection of books and magazines. New releases in fashion, photography, architecture, design, and art are presented alongside vintage stock; intuitive display compositions set a new book about Sonia Delaunay and fashion alongside a little-known novel by Marguerite Duras, a vintage Chagall catalog, and/or a Cocteau poster. There's probably an exhibition on in the gallery out the back. Or maybe a concert. Or a sale of vintage rugs or workwear. Later a vernissage—open to all—might morph into an improvised block party.

←
"We also publish postcards. It's a good way to meet young people; if I sense that there's potential, we do a postcard. It's the beginning of a dialogue. And it's important that there's something available for one euro."

↓
In the middle of the shop, a table displays some other non-publishing projects they have fun with, "little challenges to stay alert," like scented candles or ceramics.

→ A display of the artist catalogs Ofr. published to accompany their favorite exhibitions.

Ofr. has been dedicated to independent publishing and independent ideas since 1996. Set up by brother and sister duo Marie and Alexandre Thumerelle with "zero francs"—hence the name—Ofr.'s first project was publishing a free weekly guide to Paris called *Pretexte*: "the idea was not to talk about the piece of theater that we recommend you go and see, it was mostly a pretext to write things that were important to us." This then grew into a distribution service for local cultural free press, but also hard-to-find indie mags from overseas, like *The Face*, *Dazed & Confused*, *Sleazenation*, or *Ray Gun*. Ofr. truly came into their own when they opened their first shop on the Canal Saint-Martin in 1999, before moving to their current space in 2007. Today Ofr. is still a pretext; a generous, sincere and joyful ploy for Alexandre and Marie to invent the life they want.

Marie & Alexandre Thumerelle   171

←
A gallery and
event space
at the back
of the shop is
constantly being
reconfigured
to accommo-
date that week's
program. They
might be sell-
ing Moroccan
rugs, vintage
workwear, or
presenting a new
exhibition, or all
three.

↓
Ofr. is constantly on the lookout for vintage stock like these framed art posters, displayed and for sale above the shop's art section.

From the beginning with nos catalogue, published, and distributed local and foreign indie press. They have always been a major distributor of Paris fashion magazine *Purple* — "they established their own aesthetic poetry. They discovered a lot of photographers, a lot of stylists, a lot of writers who were not visible before. They were involved in the emergence of a whole scene."

→ Alexandre made a diagrammatic "constellation" of everyone they had exhibited in a single year. The poster in front of that is a souvenir of a weekend spent at his cousin's place in the country. In front of that, another diagram by Alexandre maps the scope of their activity, encompassing a publishing arm, the bookshop, the gallery, artist residencies, and a ton of other projects. They never stop!

Describe your atelier or office.
There's no office, no computer; I have a smart phone. We don't
need a computer, because in the end we prefer to meet people.
They come with a suitcase, they show us what they do, and we
look at the person too. It's also about starting a relationship
with them.

What's a typical day for you?
We open very early, at 8:30 in the morning. It's no sacrifice; we take
our kids to school and we open. Friends pass by, we drink coffee,
we talk about exhibitions we can do, books we can do, books
they've made that we can sell here, shops we could open. Generally,
and that's also why we love this neighborhood, the people who
come and drink coffee here are also passionate people, people who
have stories to tell, people who have desires, who have projects,
and who do them.

What inspires you?
Everything we publish, everything we distribute, everything we do,
each time there is this vibration, this pulsation, this enthusiasm
that says, "Let's go!" And it's worth it. You never know exactly how
things will turn out at the end, but it's worth a try anyway.

What is your motto?
Now Ofr. means "Open, Free, and Ready." I was proud to come up
with that because for fifteen years we never knew what to answer
when people asked us what Ofr. meant. We've also done several
group shows called "On Fire." I like that Jimi Hendrix song *Fire*.
It's something that at the same time resonates with me from when
I was young, in my youthful desire, and at the same time, something I hope I can transmit to other people.

Why Paris?
The place where I saw a little opening, a little fire, a little love,
a little sensuality, a little suspense—it was Paris. Suddenly I saw
people who lived differently, where conversations didn't only
revolve around the weather. Of course, you can find that in the
countryside too.... I like places where suddenly there is room
for discussion, for projects, for dreams, where there is room for
the heart.

What is unique about Paris?
The Paris we love is the Paris of artists, the Paris where things are
possible, the Paris that is open socially, open religiously, open in
terms of families. Where things are possible, where we can express
ourselves, where we're not trying to become billionaires. The Paris
of freedom.

Marie & Alexandre Thumerelle   175

VISIT

Ofr.
20 rue Dupetit-Thouars,
75003 Paris
Carreau du Temple,
METRO: Temple
Instagram: @ofrparis

THE NEIGHBORHOOD

Sandwiched in between Place de la République and the northern Marais, Ofr. is located in a micro-quarter surrounding a nineteenth-century covered market called Le Carreau du Temple from which it takes its name. "Carreau du Temple is our neighborhood today, it's where we put all our energy, we live next door, our children go to school here, it's really our base. When we moved in, the shops cost nothing; the owner was trying to find a tenant for this space for two years! The Carreau du Temple was completely abandoned. But the shops all sold one after the other to new people—young, dynamic people, and there were happy faces in the street again. And now people say, 'It's not bad after all!'"

Marie & Alexandre Thumerelle —

AGNÈS B.
Designer, gallerist
Agnès b.

↑
"I work around this table with the team—a team that I like a lot and who I love working with. We work a lot by instinct. I like to do things spontaneously. I believe in spontaneity." Hanging over the back of a chair, waiting for its hem to be repaired, the Agnès b. "Insta dress" adorned with a patchwork of photos taken from Agnès's Instagram account offers a glimpse into her world. "I think I'm the first to make a garment with an Instagram on it. It's fun."

For over forty years, fashion label Agnès b. has materialized French chic and nonchalance. In the image of their emblematic striped cotton T-shirts, recycled for each collection in a new color palette, their understated collections are designed to slot casually into any wardrobe and be worn season after season.

Punning on the French word for fashion designer, "styliste," Agnès has always defended "style" over the hallowed arena of "fashion." Her first pieces were inspired by military or work wear or other generic designs that she would reinterpret in different colors or with adjusted cuts, like a pair of over-alls in white or a reboot of traditional Chinese work wear. Her democratic, down-to-earth attitude was fully in tune with the spirit of the times, which she manifested with great vision in her now legendary first boutique that opened in 1975 inside an old butcher shop on the poetically named rue du Jour in the Les Halles quarter. There Agnès set up a freewheeling, bohemian retail experiment, a hybrid shop, office, studio, and home where her children, clients, left-wing militants, philoso-phers, artists, musicians, and friends like Félix Guattari, Gilles Deleuze, Robert Malaval, or Jean-Charles de Castelbajac would walk in off the street to cultivate ideas and friendships beneath a poster of Chairman Mao, a rainbow of ruffled skirts hanging from the butcher's hooks on the walls, and birds that were left free to fly about.

↑
A corner of her studio filled with an assortment of plants. A painting by Dalila Dalléas Bouzar titled *Lucien* hangs on the wall. "A young North African artist who sets up her easel in the street and paints people who come to pose for her. I like them a lot."

→
Agnès buys art all the time. These two recent acquisitions leaning against the wall are by the French photographer François Prost from his series "After Party"—facades of regional discos and nightclubs during the day around France and Belgium. Hanging on the wall above the orchid, two pieces by the American street art duo Skewville. "I have work to do discovering new artists for the gallery. And when I come across works that move me I buy them. It's like saying, 'Keep going, I believe in you.'"

When her fashion label started gaining international traction in the 1980s, with shops opening around the globe from New York to Tokyo, Agnès's creative ambitions and actions multiplied too. In 1984 she bought her first piece of art, a self-portrait by Jean-Michel Basquiat, who she had met and befriended in Paris at the Yvon Lambert Gallery. And soon after she opened a gallery herself, Galerie du Jour, "a place to show the hidden and the other side of things." In parallel to her engagement with contemporary art and artists, Agnès has an ongoing passion for cinema articulated via her production company Love Streams. In 2014 she even directed her own road movie, *My Name Is Hmmm….*

For over four decades Agnès b. the person and Agnès b. her company have demonstrated unwavering commitment to radical ideals of creativity, generosity, dialogue, and political engagement, the breeding ground for the best French style.

↓
A view of Agnès's desk. The feather will be used as inspiration for a new print. "We work a lot in digital."

Describe your profession.
Fashion designer. That's what's on my passport.

Your favorite tool?
Before I had a thirty-five millimeter Nikon, now I have a digital
Nikon camera, or I use my phone.

What's a typical day for you?
In the morning I like to work in my head alone at home. It's the only
time of the day where I'm a little quiet. I like my house in the morning, to move things around. I have a very autobiographical house.
There are things from my family from Versailles that have been in my
family for a very long time, and then a drawing by Basquiat, a photo
by Nan Goldin, and heaps of paintings, mostly contemporary. I live
outside Paris, so I leave around 11 in the morning and arrive at the
studio around 12:30, then I might work until 10 p.m. or later.

What is your favorite neighborhood in Paris?
I love Paris tremendously. I like the Canal Saint-Martin; we were
pioneers here too. The Canal is such a pretty place. And so lively.

What is luxury?
I don't like luxury so much. I find it a bit obscene in this day and
age. A 3,500 euro handbag! I find that weird. I wonder if we need
that? If it's to show that we can afford it; that principle alone is a
little sickening. For me luxury is time. It's the light. It's my garden.

↑
"Before I drew, but I don't have time. So I take pictures,
it's faster." As much as her drawings, Agnès's photographs
are at the center of her creative process. They are used
as inspiration for a new season's color palette, are printed
on fabric and transformed into garments, are made into
postcards. She also likes to shoot the collections.

← Agnès's phone with a case inspired by brass knuckles she picked up in the streets of New York.

↓ In 1996 Agnès published *Des photographes et le cardigan pression*, in which she invited sixty-five photographers, from Claude Lévêque to Dominique Issermann, to contribute an image inspired by her emblematic snap cardigan.

↑
Where it all began for Agnès b.: Facing the Saint-Eustache church in the heart of the Les Halles quarter, the original boutique at Nº 3 is today dedicated to their men's collections. When she opened there in 1975, Les Halles was in the midst of being gutted, as the centuries-old food market there was moved out to the suburbs and a new shopping and transport hub developed in its place. The Agnès b. boutique was a pioneering experiment in retail which declared shops as a space for expression and encounters. To this day, when you drop in to any one of the Agnès b. boutiques around Paris or elsewhere you'll probably find an exhibition on the walls, a film poster in the window, and cool music on the sound system.

→
A trace of the hand, of humanity, Agnès's handwriting is omnipresent in her company: from the logo, to signage around the company headquarters, to the labels on the clothes. "I have very simple handwriting actually, I haven't changed my style since the age of twelve I think." Here, using a Krink marker by her friend the graffiti artist Craig Costello, Agnès draws the logo for her art journal *le point d'ironie*. She came across the symbol in an old Larousse encyclopedia and learned it was a punctuation mark invented by the French writer Alcanter de Brahm at the end of the nineteenth century to indicate ironic passages in a text.

→
The first issue of the free art pamphlet *le point d'iro-nie* Agnès created after a discussion with her friends the artist Christian Boltanski and the art critic Hans-Ulrich Obrist in 1997. Obrist remains the editor in chief. Every two months or so an artist is given carte blanche to make the folded A2 sheet his or her own, then 100,000 copies are distributed around the world. A free work of art for all! For this, the first issue, Agnès's friend, the experimental filmmaker Jonas Mekas presented his "Anti-100 Years of Cinema Manifesto."

I WAS THERE WITH MY CAMERA MY HEART BEATING QUICKLY
WITH EXCITEMENT - LIFE, LIFE, HERE + NOW - AS MY CAMERA
BUZZED . I WAS OUT OF MY MIND AND IN ECSTASY - AH, MY
DEAR FRIENDS - THESE FRAGMENTS OF PARADISE - - - - -

Carl Th. Dreyer, New York, September 17, 1965 (from WALDEN)   siesta time, cassis, Summer 1966. (from NOTES FOR JEROME)

ah! Mayakovski,
Sandburg!
I never understood
your craze for
technology --

ah! Mayakovski

Self-portrait, 1975 (from HE STANDS IN A DESERT COUNTING THE   picking wild strawberries at Willard Van Dyke's place, Vermont, June 24, 1978
SECONDS OF HIS LIFE)   (from HE STANDS IN A DESERT COUNTING THE SECONDS OF HIS LIFE)

VISIT

La Fab.
1 place Jean-Michel Basquiat,
75013 Paris
Bibliothèque, METRO: Bibliothèque
François Mitterand
www.lafab.net

THE FOUNDATION

In late 2019 Agnès inaugurated La Fab., an acronym for the Fondation Agnès b. It's a proper public home for her foundation and ever-growing art collection. La Fab. is located opposite the landmark National Library of France in the popular 13th arrondissement, inside a new building located on the place Jean-Michel Basquiat, an address Agnès took as a sign and a blessing. Her collection started with a self-portrait by Basquiat, and demonstrates all the personality of something assembled with instinct and passion, taking in street art, video, photography, sculpture, and everything in between, and includes works by, to cite just a few, Harmony Korine, Nan Goldin, Martin Parr, Malick Sidibé, Ryan McGinley, JonOne, Louise Bourgeois, Andy Warhol, and Simon Hantaï. La Fab. is also home to her Galerie du Jour, so in addition to themed exhibitions sourced from the collection, the space presents new works by different artists they support. There's a bookshop too, and space for the foundation's humanitarian and ecological actions.

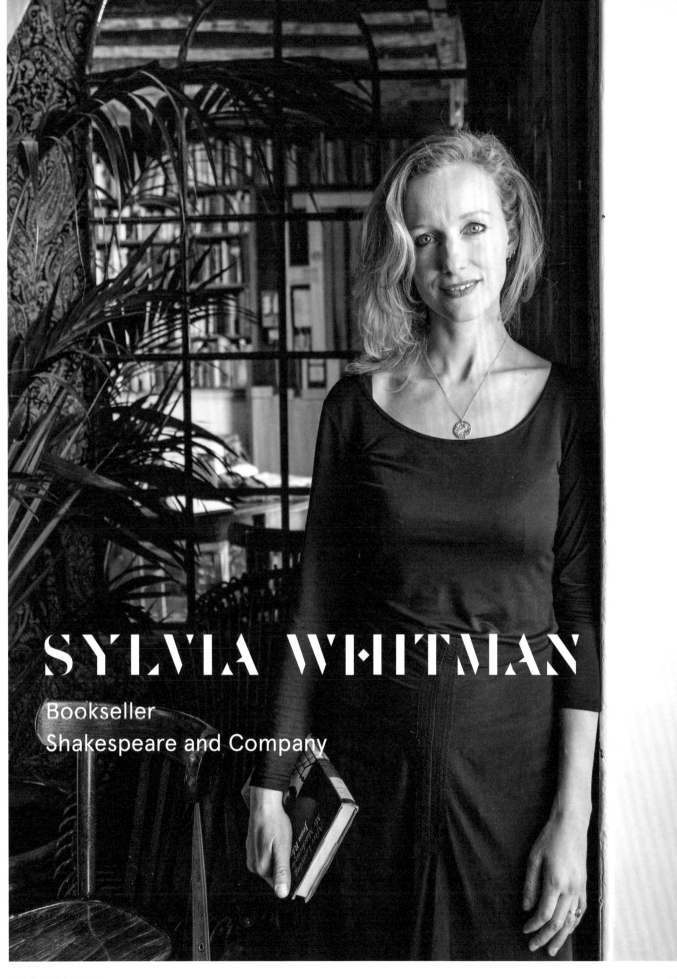

SYLVIA WHITMAN

Bookseller
Shakespeare and Company

Shakespeare and Company, the legendary English-language bookshop on Paris's Left Bank, has been a beacon for artists, writers, bohemians, and all sorts of other dreamers and freaks since George Whitman first opened its doors in 1951. Sylvia, his only child, joined George at the bookshop in 2002 after graduating from university in London; apart from her early years in Paris, she grew up in the UK with her English mother. In 2006 George officially handed over the reins to her, just a few years before he passed away in his bedroom above the shop, two days after his ninety-eighth birthday.

Much of George's long life was dedicated to running his little "rag and bone shop of the heart" as he liked to call the bookshop, quoting the last two lines of a favorite poem by Yeats. He constructed his kingdom as one might write a novel, wanting people to open the door of the shop "the way they open a book; a book that leads into a magic world in their imaginations."

Located on the banks of the Seine facing Notre Dame and vibrating with its own sort of bohemian feng shui, the bookshop sits on a tiny little square festooned with string lights and featuring one of Paris's beautiful nineteenth-century public water fountains. Stands of secondhand books are wheeled out the front. And you might see the shop dog, Colette, or the adopted stray cat, Aggie, hanging about. On the left, a wooden bench for readers sits in front of the shop's antiquarian book department, dedicated to first editions and other rare books. And next to that is the café that Sylvia opened in 2015, fulfilling a dream George had had since the 1960s. Tables spill out in front, overlooking the cathedral and the beautiful Square René-Viviani (with the oldest tree in Paris, planted in 1601), the river and its *bouquinistes*.

For over sixty years, Shakespeare and Company has been at the heart of literary life in Paris, generously joining the dots between books, readers, and writers. With her partner David Delannet, Sylvia continues to run the bookshop in the same spirit as her father, fostering a culture of sharing, reading, writing, and lots of fun! Here, to quote George, "the business of books is the business of life!"

↑
"When I'm thinking about Dad I often go and pick up *Leaves of Grass*, there's something about this humanitarian voice: everyone is equal, even a blade of grass is important. Dad loved Whitman's poetry, but he also really loved the person that he was. My dad was like this in his own way, because he had his door constantly open. George feels like a daily presence here, a daily inspiration, his spirit still feels very much a part of the walls. I also really miss his eccentricity; I miss having that daily contact with someone who is totally mad!"

→
With the motto "Be not inhospitable to strangers lest they be angels in disguise," and in recognition of the generosity he himself encountered when he traveled through the US as a young man, George offered a bed to writers, artists, and thinkers passing through Paris. In exchange, each Tumbleweed, as they are called, was asked to write a one-page autobiography for the shop's archives, read a book a day, and help out in the shop. Shakespeare and Company estimates that the bookshop has hosted 30,000 Tumbleweeds since it opened in 1951. Sylvia continues the tradition. Up to four people continue to bed down in the shop every night. Sylvia remembers as a child stepping over often hungover Tumbleweeds on the shop floor in the morning, up to eighteen at a time, with her father shouting "Up you get! Rise and shine!" Says Sylvia: "It was a real scene." The website makes clear today that "the charm of the Tumbleweed program lies in its communal nature ... privacy is not really an option!"

BE NOT INHOSPITABLE TO STRANGERS
LEST THEY BE ANGELS IN DISGUISE

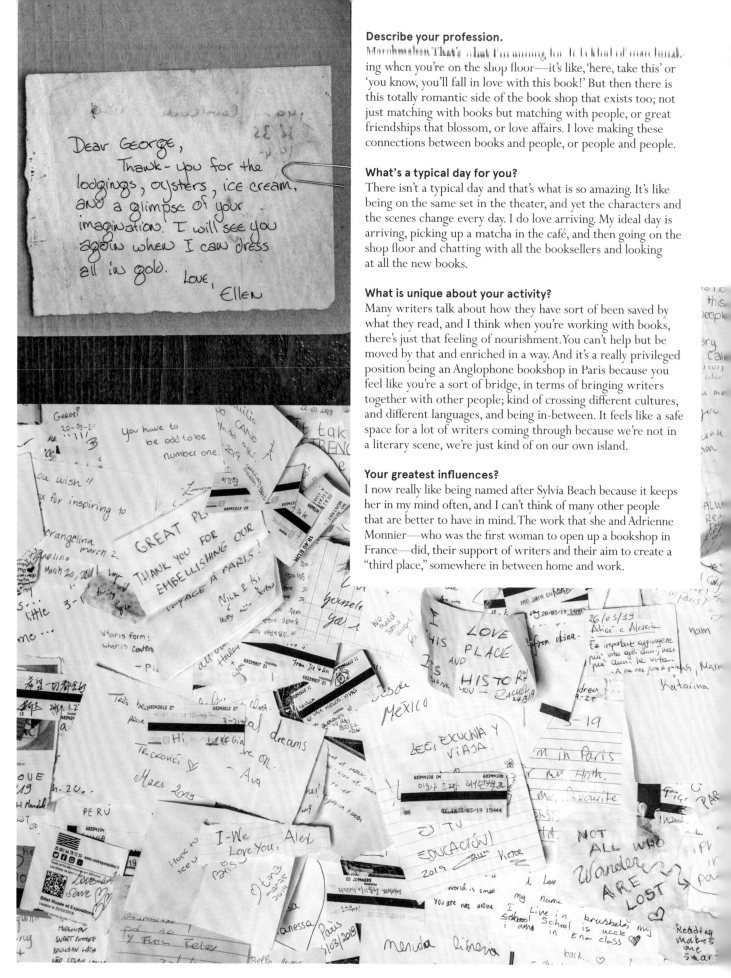

Describe your profession.

Matchmaker. That's what I'm aiming for. It's kind of matchmaking when you're on the shop floor—it's like, 'here, take this' or 'you know, you'll fall in love with this book!' But then there is this totally romantic side of the book shop that exists too; not just matching with books but matching with people, or great friendships that blossom, or love affairs. I love making these connections between books and people, or people and people.

What's a typical day for you?

There isn't a typical day and that's what is so amazing. It's like being on the same set in the theater, and yet the characters and the scenes change every day. I do love arriving. My ideal day is arriving, picking up a matcha in the café, and then going on the shop floor and chatting with all the booksellers and looking at all the new books.

What is unique about your activity?

Many writers talk about how they have sort of been saved by what they read, and I think when you're working with books, there's just that feeling of nourishment. You can't help but be moved by that and enriched in a way. And it's a really privileged position being an Anglophone bookshop in Paris because you feel like you're a sort of bridge, in terms of bringing writers together with other people; kind of crossing different cultures, and different languages, and being in-between. It feels like a safe space for a lot of writers coming through because we're not in a literary scene, we're just kind of on our own island.

Your greatest influences?

I now really like being named after Sylvia Beach because it keeps her in my mind often, and I can't think of many other people that are better to have in mind. The work that she and Adrienne Monnier—who was the first woman to open up a bookshop in France—did, their support of writers and their aim to create a "third place," somewhere in between home and work.

What is your motto?

I like "Give what you can, take what you need," which is really connected to the Tumbleweeds sleeping in the bookshop. And "Be not inhospitable to strangers, lest they be angels in disguise" has gained more weight with me with age, and with what's going on with the refugee crisis.

Why Paris?

For the same reason my father gave: "Paris—where poetry is part of life; where men are poets and life is a poem." As a bookstore you feel at home. There is such a presence and appreciation of books here. The river is lined with bouquinistes, and there are hundreds and hundreds of independent bookstores.

Your favorite tool?

A book! Umberto Eco said that the book is like "the spoon, scissors, the hammer, the wheel. Once invented, it cannot be improved."

A life-changing meeting?

Jeanette Winterson. I first met her in 2007 when my father hit her over the head with a book thrown from his third-floor window; she and I have been friends ever since. Her friendship is one full of humor, love, and finding solutions to things we both care about: words, people, and the dog Colette. And, separate from that, her books are my daily compass for living.

↓
Added to the Tumbleweeds sleeping on the first floor, George's former apartment on the third floor is reserved for the stream of authors invited to participate in the shop's busy program of events and book signings. "There is such a specific atmosphere that is created by having people sleeping here, who are here just for literature and have such excitement about being in Paris for literary reasons. It keeps that flame going. And you can feel it when you come in; you can sense this source of energy."

←
Since Sylvia took over from her father, she has expanded the bookshop into a jumble of adjacent spaces. "For the first time I'm like this is a good size for poetry, this is a good size for the art section. It no longer feels frustrating trying to squeeze in all the books. At first I though it was probably not good business to expand the poetry section, but it's been like bees to honey. There's a real buzz around poetry at the moment."

→
After a Tumbleweed complained that there was no private space to write in the bookshop, George built a little nook at the top of the stairs in the first-floor library and put a typewriter there.

↑

"The story I love the most is this 1958 meeting that took place here with Allen Ginsberg, Gregory Corso, and William Burroughs. It was this kind of wild happening where Corso and Ginsberg took their clothes off to read their poetry, and Burroughs read from *Naked Lunch* for the first time. Dad said no one knew whether to laugh or be sick."

Sylvia Whitman

VISIT

Shakespeare and Company
37 rue de la Bûcherie,
75005 Paris
Latin Quarter, METRO: Saint-Michel
www.shakespeareandcompany.com

MUST BUY

In 2016 Shakespeare and Company published the first book about the history of the bookshop, *Shakespeare and Company, Paris: A History of the Rag & Bone Shop of the Heart*. It includes many treasures from the shop's voluminous archive, including photographs and original Tumbleweed autobiographies, as well as contributions from writers such as Allen Ginsberg, Anaïs Nin, Kate Tempest, Ethan Hawke, and Jeanette Winterson.

Sylvia Whitman —

ISABEL MARANT

Fashion designer
Isabel Marant

The ultimate Paris poster girl, Isabel Marant incarnates a certain bohemian *je ne sais quoi*. A typical look might match a pair of cropped straight leg jeans or a miniskirt with a peasant blouse, a tailored jacket embellished with a Navajo motif or Rajasthani-style fringe, and a pair of studded ankle boots. Her ensembles all have a signature slouch, at once sexy and a bit boyish. "Never design anything you wouldn't wear yourself," she was advised when studying fashion at Paris's Studio Berçot in the mid-1980s, and she has made this her credo.

After graduating, Isabel racked up a few early jobs in fashion before quickly striking out on her own, driven by a creative and entrepreneurial spirit she inherited from her parents. She started out with accessories, then in 1990 set up a short-lived knitwear line in collaboration with her mother, a former model who ran a fashion boutique in Saint-Germain-des-Prés at the time. In 1994, Isabel launched her own-name label, with a first show the following year, where she sent out a bunch of her girlfriends to parade her designs in the courtyard of an artists' squat. If Helmut Lang was at the height of his fame at the time, defining the decade with an intellectual, avant-garde minimalism, Isabel was designing collections she wanted to wear herself, rooted in a day-to-day urban reality. She injected a touch of carefree chic to Paris fashion week, combining loose, comfortable fabrics, sportswear, workwear, and vintage influences with far-flung touches and a playful color palette. These elements remain at the heart of the brand's DNA today.

For over twenty-five years, Isabel has built her empire brick by brick, a slow-burn driving the brand toward a constant ascent. A collaboration in the late aughts with the stylist Emmanuelle Alt, editor-in-chief of *Vogue Paris* since 2011, injected extra glamour into the house's boho style, helping put her on the map internationally. Then in 2013, her wildly successful H&M capsule made her a household name.

Today, Isabel Marant remains her own first and best client. With her salt-and-pepper hair casually pulled up in a topknot, no makeup to speak of, a ready smile beaming out through the wafts of smoke from one of her little roll-your-own cigarettes as she zips around Paris on her Vespa, she incarnates her own version of the modern woman, making tangible, like all fashion designers must, the attitudes and tempo of her generation.

Isabel working in her studio. "I do sketches of the general direction of the collection, more like a storyboard, then I immediately get down to the tangible, to something in three dimensions with the fabric, because I find that the relationship between the shape, the fall of a fabric, a colour—that's what results in something in the end."

Isabel Marant

Describe your office?

It's a big open space, very messy, with lots of things lying around because I need to have a lot of different things around that catch my eye and that my mind can bounce off. I don't work much with the computer. I need plenty of daylight because I spend my time choosing colors and textures. I always work to music. Music is really important for the energy, the rhythm of a collection. I listen to a bit of everything but always things with a good beat. A fair bit of hip-hop, funk, trap.... I listen to a lot of the same music as my 16-year-old son Tal.

Your style?

I have always taken the word "ready-to-wear" literally. What interests me is to dress real people and not to make clothes for special occasions, red carpet, or whatever. What has always motivated me in my creations is the question, "What am I going to wear today?" I want to be at ease in my clothes, because I think we are always attracted to things that we feel good in, that are comfortable, easy to care for, and not a kind of straitjacket that you can't move in. And I like a woman to *avoir du chien*. I'm not sure how to translate that. In French, to "have some dog" is an expression that for me conveys something quite subtle between cool, elegant, and unpretentious but still noticeable.

What inspires you?

It can start from anything. In general, it's something very tenuous. It could be a pink Post-it on the ground, or a woman who lifts her hair and all of a sudden I say to myself, "A woman's neck is really very pretty." It could be a word, a thing. I often give the example of a cook who has different ingredients and who doesn't really know what dish she will make. It's a bit like that for me. I accumulate little ingredients that appeal to me in a very instinctive way then I start trying to understand what they all mean together. It's always very light, very abstract to begin with, then becomes something precise and concrete.

Your heritage?

I feel deeply French but inspired by the cultures of the world that are then reinterpreted by my Parisian point of view. I was raised by a very French father, a kind of Jean Gabin type, but my mother is German, and my father remarried a West Indian woman. So I have this very French side, but very multicultural at the same time.

What's a typical day for you?

It's a race from start to finish. Usually I arrive early, I get to the office at 8 a.m. because it gives me an hour and a half to think a little about things before everyone arrives, and usually every other day I stay late. During the day, it's nonstop meetings with the different teams to develop and perfect our different products, quite intense technical stuff. So at the end of the day I need to reboot my brain and put things back in place and try to find solutions to the different problems that came up throughout the day.

How do you explain your success?

Many different women dress in my clothes, it goes from my mother, to my grandmother, to my niece. It's trans-generational, and that's something I'm extremely proud of. I also make clothes that are adapted to the way we live today, that are easy to take care of, that don't need ironing, that can be put in the washing machine. And also I have been able to create a style which has remained the same since the beginning.

What is unique about your work?

What is really stimulating in fashion is all the trades that revolve around fashion, all the crafts like lace, weaving, embroidery, feather artisans. Fashion may be an industry, but it is nevertheless an extremely artisanal one. It's really one of the parts of my job that I like the most. That's why I have always loved knits, because there is that very artisanal aspect to them. I like that from a single thread we can create hundreds of different things.

Isabel Marant   197

←
If some garments can be created with flat pattern-making techniques, other designs are composed in muslin directly onto a mannequin, using a technique known as draping. It allows you to immediately see how the design looks in volume and make easy adjustments. If the garment is symmetrical, draping is done only on the right side of the form. The two mm-wide blue draping tape indicates the edges of each piece of fabric; once the design is perfected, the different pieces will serve as the base for the patternmaker. The workshop is populated with these industry standard Siegel & Stockman manne-quins that are handcrafted from recycled paper covered in calico in a workshop near Paris.

↓
After the design, patternmaking, and fabric cutting, the machinist stitches the different elements together to produce the finished garment.

　　　Isabel Marant

↑
Part of a dressmaker's arsenal: pins, scissors, blue draping tape, professional pattern weights, and the graders set square for pattern-cutting with the seam allowance marked in orange.

↑
New shoe models for the SS20 collection in the showroom. These ankle boots have a graphic shape enhanced by the label's signature triangular heel and pointed toe. The essential accessory to complete the Isabel Marant look, the shoe collections are a huge success for the label, always reliably walkable, but cool and sexy too. The wedge high-top they launched in 2009 took all the comfort of the sneaker and added a dose of glamour and sex appeal, and has been endlessly copied around the world.

Isabel Marant
354 rue Saint-Honoré, 75001 Paris
Louvre, METRO: Concorde or Tuileries
www.isabelmarant.com

PARIS BOUTIQUES

In 1998, three years after her first fashion show, Isabel opened a shop on rue de Charonne, in the popular Bastille neighborhood. In the slipstream of Jean-Paul Gaultier, who had set up his HQ nearby a couple of years earlier, she brought some fashion cred to this indie neighborhood populated with artists of all kinds who had been slowly taking over workshops left empty by departing artisans. "We opened in this neighborhood because it was full of furniture makers and all sorts of other artisans and craftspeople working in bronze, gilding, silverware, etc. I have always loved the whole Bastille and Faubourg-Saint-Antoine district for all the very French artisanal *savoir faire* there." The spirit of a neighborhood remains just as important to Isabel today, and she now counts five boutiques scattered throughout Paris, including the newest on rue Saint-Honoré, halfway between Place Vendôme and the Tuileries Garden. And in 2019, the label's first dedicated menswear store opened in the Northern Marais. Isabel has always paid special attention to the window displays of all her boutiques too, collaborating with artist Arnold Goron on eye-catching installations, often incorporating kinetic art and sculpture and inspired by each new collection.

ANDRÉ SARAIVA

Artist, hotelier, entrepreneur
Amour Hotels

André Saraiva's winking stick figure, Mr. A, is tagged on walls from Venice Beach, California, to Venice, Italy, and downtown New York to the streets of Lisbon. André started his career as a graffiti artist in Paris in the late 1980s and has since brought his elegant outlaw approach to projects ranging from nightclubs, cafés, magazines, shops, and hotels, but also to the service of brands, from *Peanuts* to Absolut. "I never asked permission. I did all this business without being a businessman. Nobody said, 'Oh, I'm gonna help you' or 'I'm giving you money.' I'm not waiting for you to give me permission to come and play in your courtyard. I just come; I squat."

Born in Uppsala, Sweden, to Portuguese parents who had fled their country's Estado Novo regime, André moved to Paris with his family as a ten-year-old in 1981. A few years later he was running alongside artists like Invader and Zevs (see them at work in Banksy's 2010 cult documentary, or prank, *Exit Through the Gift Shop*) as part of the first generation of the Parisian street art scene, tagging the city not with his name, but with his cheeky Mr. A character.

In 1996 André married his art to retail, opening an experimental pop-up shop in Paris, the Mercier d'André, where he sold his paintings by the meter and got friends involved to make a sort of happening. He credits a shift in thinking, where "a place was almost like doing a painting or a piece of art. But with more dimension." When the radical arts space the Palais de Tokyo reopened in 2002, André and some friends set up an innovative retail space there called BlackBlock that sold all sorts of artist's editions and objects.

If so much of André's energy has been dedicated to fashioning something out of the zeitgeist, Paris is lucky to be home to two of his more enduring projects. In 2006, André and two other associates opened the first Hôtel Amour in the Little Athens quarter below Pigalle, a boutique hotel like no other that combines fair prices, inspired décor, and a special atmosphere. A decade later its sister address opened near Gare de l'Est. Both hotels' restaurants and bars are always overflowing with a fun and international bohemian set. André explains, "It's about the people. The people who stay there, who live there, who eat there, who make love there. That's what makes a place."

↑
Pink is André's favorite color and his lavish use of it in his graffiti has always set him apart. "Pink makes all the other colors look good." From his "love graffitis"—a project where he took commissions to tag a loved one's name in the street—to his love hotels, André has never pushed the typical message of an urban outlaw; rather he's always advocated love, sensuality, and fun. "Love is maybe the most important value for humanity; it makes us do stuff."

→
André's signature tag is his cheeky alter ego, Mr. A, a rakish, long-limbed stick figure wearing a top hat with a circle and a cross for eyes. "I used to just write my name on walls but I wanted to find a signature that would speak to more people, that everybody could understand. How can I do a figure with great economy, with as few lines as possible but still expressive. That's when Mr. A was born."

→→
The corridors of the Hôtel Grand Amour are carpeted with two custom motifs André designed with one of France's oldest furnishing manufacturers, Maison Pierre Frey. Take your pick between the blue floors carpeted with a motif of stylized vulvas, eyes, and mouths, and the pink floors covered with a phallic floral design. The carpets underscore the hotel's playful and sexy vibe.

André Saraiva   203

Describe your profession
It all started with me writing my name on walls. Thirty years later
I still do the same thing; I've just expanded the scope to different
surfaces.

What's a typical day for you?
There's no typical day. Most of my days are totally different
depending on which city I'm in and what project I'm working on.
That makes it exciting, but sometimes I miss a little routine.

What's your favorite hiding place?
A bed in a hotel where I'm staying under an alias.

Your favorite tool?
My marker.

What is your favorite neighborhood in Paris?
I think Paris is amazing and like all good cities, every neighborhood
has its own life and story. I love the 10th because it's in the center
of Paris, but you still have a mix of nationalities and social classes,
and you still find some of the old institutions and shops that are
the heart of Paris.

Your greatest influences?
I've always admired a lot of artists and I've met a few people in
my life who were really inspiring. He's dead now but I love Glenn
O'Brien. He was a writer and intellectual and he had a TV show
on the public channel in New York called *TV Party* that was very
underground, very interesting.

What is unique about your work?
Putting people together at the Factory was part of Andy Warhol's
art. I think art is not just doing a painting or an installation in a
gallery and hoping the good collectors and the good museums
buy you. That's still working for someone; I don't like to work for
anyone. Graffiti gave me the freedom to not be accepted by anyone;
you just do it for the pleasure and the story you want to tell.

What is your motto?
"All is for the best in the best of all worlds."

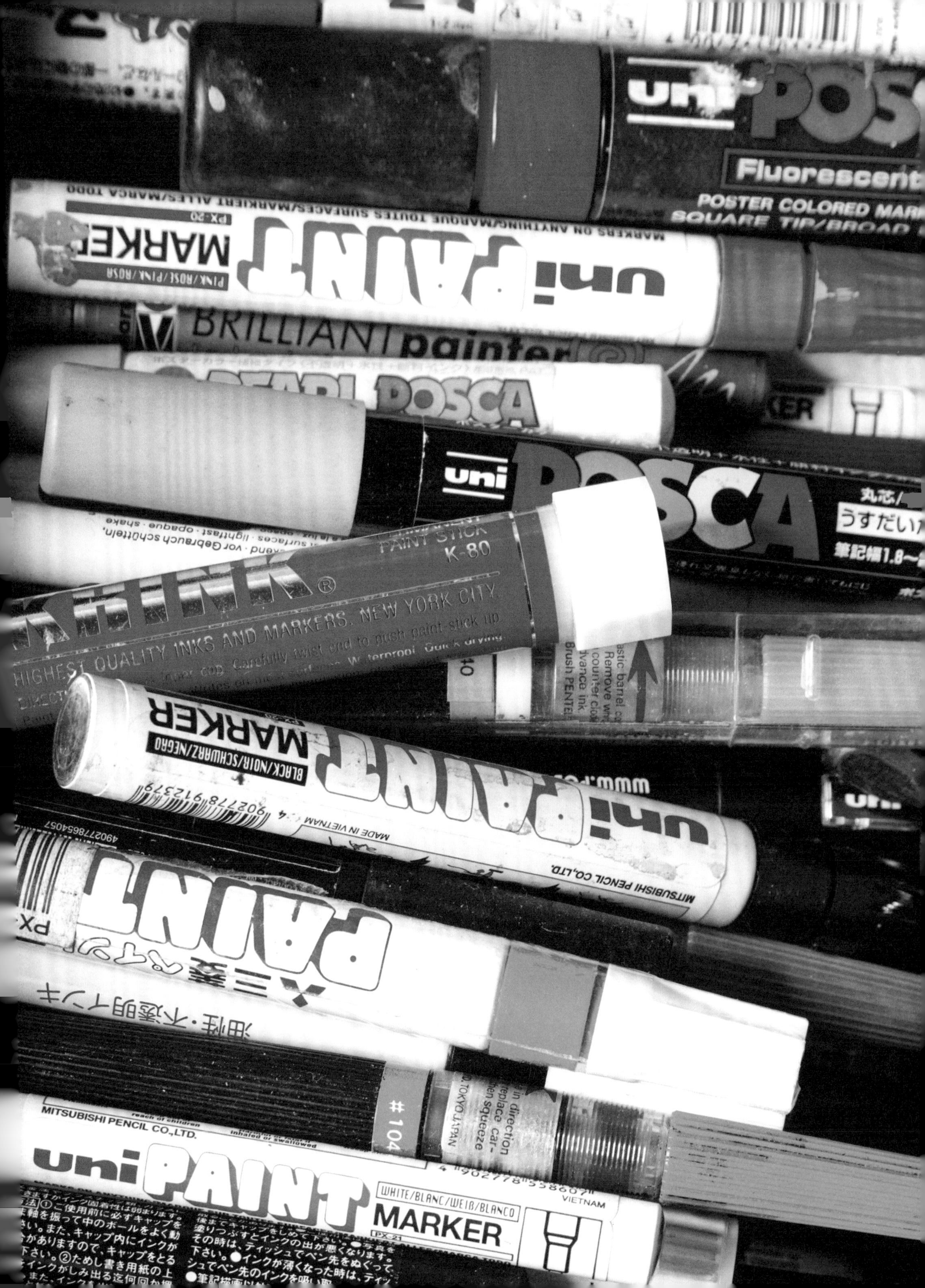

uni POSCA

Fluorescent

POSTER COLORED MARKER
SQUARE TIP/BROAD

MARKERS ON ANYTHING/MARQUE TOUTES SURFACES/MARKIERT ALLES/MARCA 1000

PX-20

uni PAINT MARKER

PINK/ROSE/PINK/ROSA

BRILLIANT painter

PEARL POSCA

uni POSCA

丸芯/
うすだい
筆記幅1.8〜

PAINT STICK K-80

KRINK ®

HIGHEST QUALITY INKS AND MARKERS. NEW YORK CITY

Carefully twist end to push paint-stick up.
Waterproof. Quick drying.

astic barrel co
Remove wh
counter cloc
dvance ink
Brush PENTE

uni PAINT MARKER

BLACK/NOIR/SCHWARZ/NEGRO

MADE IN VIETNAM

MITSUBISHI PENCIL CO.,LTD.

4 902778 912379

4902778654057

PX

uni PAINT

ペイントマーカー

油性・不透明インキ

uni

#104

in direction
replace Car-
en squeeze

TOKYO JAPAN

4 902778 558607

VIETNAM

MITSUBISHI PENCIL CO.,LTD.
reach of children
inhaled or swallowed

uni PAINT MARKER

WHITE/BLANC/WEIB/BLANCO

PX-21

法①ご使用前に必ずキャップ
さい。軸を振って中のボールが動
があしますとインキが出ます。キャップ内にインキが
下さい。②ためし書き用紙の上
インキがしみ出る溶付紙の上

In a corner of the Book Bar at the Hôtel Grand Amour, a mega sound system and a collection of vinyl. André was associated with the best clubs of the aughts in Paris, starting with the Baron that he took over with friends in 2003. "The night for me was the same thing as graffiti, and maybe graffiti, because I had to do it at night, opened the door to the night. I've always thought of the night not as a time but a place. People are different there. And it's a place where I felt accepted since I was very young. It was a revelation. I still love the night."

↑
When André is in Paris, he moves in to the Hôtel Grand Amour for the duration of his stay. His personal effects are stored in a wardrobe that is wheeled in to whatever room is available. This nomadic lifestyle is nothing new. "My parents are Portuguese. I was born in Sweden, and with my mom we moved around a lot when I was a kid; I never had this idea of belonging to one country or place. I always adapted to wherever I was. It was more interesting to be a bit different, and gave me a lot of freedom."

WORLD RECORD

Stuck to the side of the façade of the Hôtel Grand Amour is the "tallest Mr. A in the world," fifty-five feet (17m) tall and eight feet (2.5) wide. It's composed of 1,300 blue-and-white azulejos tiles that André hand painted in an old factory in Portugal. André first worked with the traditional Portuguese tile technique for an earlier project, a massive mural in the São Vicente de Fora quarter commissioned by the Lisbon City Council and the Design and Fashion Museum (MUDE) in 2016. Working with such a permanent, durable medium makes quite a change. "I used to paint a Mr. A, and maybe a week or even a day after it would be painted over."

Hôtel Grand Amour
18 rue de la Fidélité, 75010 Paris
Gare de l'Est, METRO: Gare de l'Est
www.hotelamourparis.fr

Hôtel Amour
8 rue de Navarin, 75009 Paris
Little Athens, METRO: Saint-Georges
www.hotelamourparis.fr

André Saraiva –

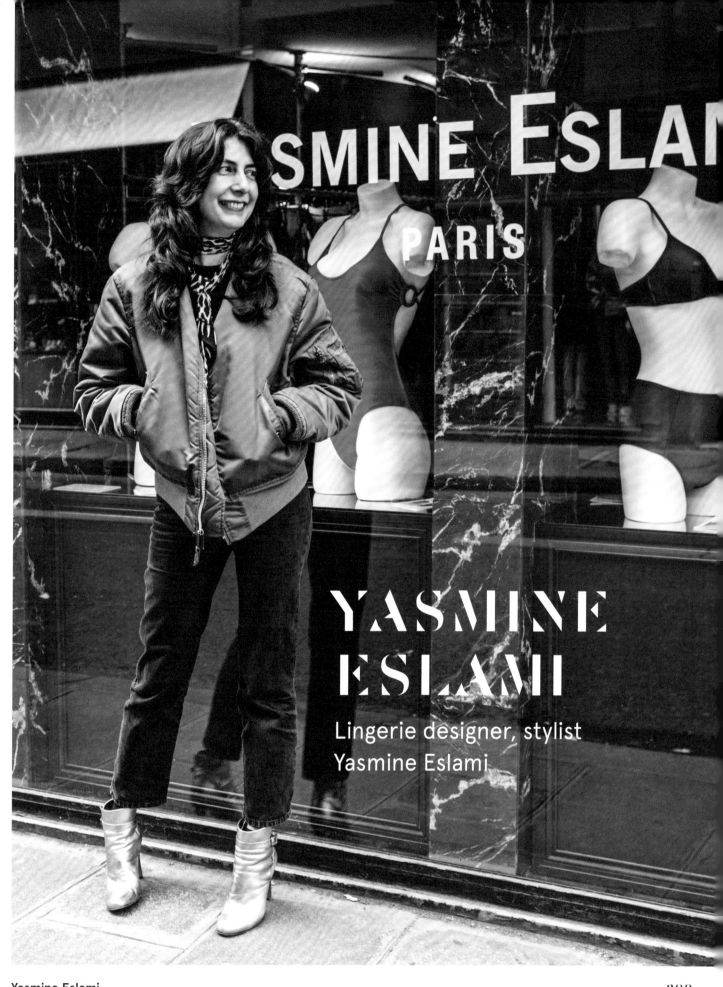

YASMINE
ESLAMI

Lingerie designer, stylist
Yasmine Eslami

Out with the frippery, the ruffles, the saccharine hues; this is lingerie of a new order. Yasmine Eslami's boutique sets the tone with a vibe that is more rock and roll than boudoir. A giant black-and-white poster of house muse Jeanne Damas is plastered over one of the black walls. Inspired by nightclub toilets, the dressing room walls are covered with graffiti tags. And by the till hangs a photo by Yasmine's friend, photographer Harry Peccinotti, that claims a certain cultural heritage: punk icon Jordan Mooney in 1979, sitting on a bed in her underwear at Vivienne Westwood and Malcom McLaren's celebrated London boutique, Sex.

Yasmine grew up in Paris and studied fashion design at Paris's famous Studio Berçot, an institution whose alumni include fashion mavens Véronique Leroy, Isabel Marant, and Martine Sitbon. After graduating, Yasmine moved to London for a summer internship with Vivienne Westwood and ended up staying a decade. She did a full 360 of the house, starting with learning how to make the perfect cuppa to being Vivienne's PA, then working on the shows and moving up to design the secondary line, Red Label. Was it here, getting up close to Westwood's iconic revamps of the corset in the 1990s that her fascination with underwear was born?

Back in Paris a decade later, Yasmine spent the aughts focused on styling, frequently working with the libidinous celebrity editor of *Purple* magazine Olivier Zahm, helping to elaborate a certain avant-garde Paris fashion attitude. (Zahm has shot every one of Eslami's lingerie campaigns.)

Another ten-year cycle later, in 2011, Eslami launched her lingerie label, "a little by chance" she says. Eslami's lingerie collections create a balance between fine, light fabrics —including Swiss cotton, Italian crepe, German technical mesh, and French lace from Calais—a subtle, modern palette, and a sleek, natural silhouette, that is sexy and French as hell!

↓
A telling stack of books and magazines: inaugural issue of *Butt* (Spring 2001) with Paris-based fashion designer Bernhard Willhelm on the cover. ("This was shot in my flat. I styled a lot for Bernhard.") Marguerite Duras is Yasmine's favorite writer. She's "read all her books many times." Early Disney is an inspiration for its subtle color palette, and it was Yasmine who suggested a collab between Pamela Anderson and Vivienne Westwood. "I love Pamela. She's a great person."

← Here different embroidered motifs are tested on a vintage bra.

↓ A big fan of French cafés, Yasmine has always liked these classic rattan bistro chairs by historic manufacturer Maison Drucker. On the floor, one of the many rugs that decorate her studio and shop. "I'm half Iranian so I was brought up with rugs. I love them because they are easy to move around and they can change a space completely and very easily."

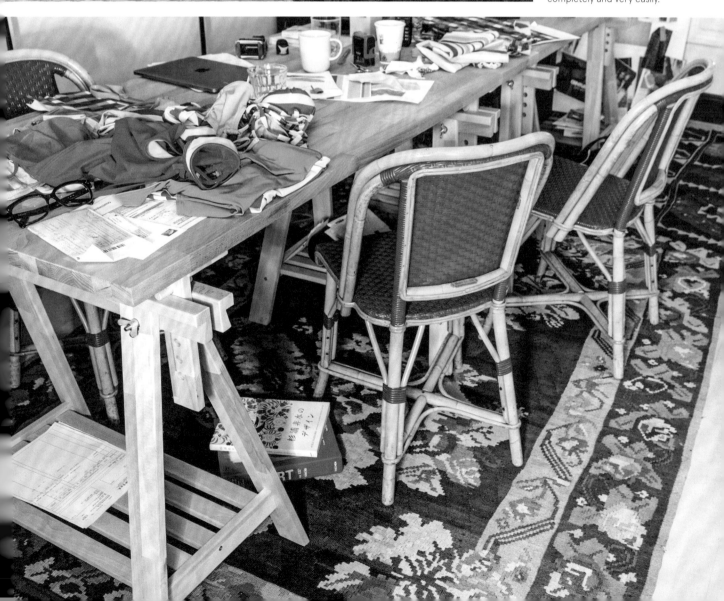

A mood board perched on a chair in the studio is covered with swatches, sketches, and pages torn out of magazines, including photos of Brigitte Bardot, who Yasmine has always loved and looked to as a source of an inspiration.

↑

This life-size paper prototype of a bathing suit in a Madras print they are developing allows the team to test the scale of the pattern against the body.

Yasmine Eslami

What is your favorite tool?
Mechanical pencil, color pencils, and notebooks—lots of them.
I like to write.

Who is your hero?
Maybe my mum :-) and Marilyn Monroe or David Bowie.

A life-changing meeting?
After I finished fashion school in Paris, I started an internship with
Vivienne Westwood. I was so happy to spend the summer in London,
but I didn't think that I would stay on for nearly ten years! At the
time, the early 1990s, it was a small team and we lived and worked
together, went out at night and spent holidays together too. I was
twenty-four hours nonstop in the Westwood world! It was my new
family. Vivienne showed me how to structure a collection, how to
think. She has done so many designs and collections and influenced
so many people, it was very special to listen to her. I worked on
so many different areas for her, starting with learning to make the
perfect cup of tea—something I didn't know at all coming from
Paris. Do you want it white or black? Sugar or not? The streets of
London and the nightlife were also a great inspiration. We used to
go to Portobello Market every weekend and find incredible stuff like
an Ossie Clark Alcantara piece for £1.50, which I wore nonstop.

What is unique about Paris?
Its size. And Parisian cafés are my absolute favorite places.

What is your favorite neighborhood in Paris?
There are so many! Montmartre, up from Pigalle or Blanche. I love
the people, the atmosphere. And I love the Palais-Royal. And the
Place du Caire is like a living postcard of old Paris.

Is there a secret to your job?
Curiosity is very important—always looking at what's going on in
the world.

What is your greatest extravagance?
Being able to do what I want.

What do you consider your greatest achievement?
Maybe stopping smoking. I still have a lot to achieve!

↑
Yasmine's essential work tools are pencils and lots of notebooks. And she
always listens to music while she works. "I love radio. I need it to work. In the
morning I like to listen to the news and then in the afternoon I switch to Fip
or Nova, or sometimes Radio Classique. Or I listen to Neil Young's *Harvest* on
repeat." She also loves to make and eat cakes, like this bowl of *chouquettes*
(balls of airy choux pastry sprinkled with pearl sugar that you can find at most
French bakeries).

VISIT

Yasmine Eslami
35 rue de Richelieu, 75001 Paris
Palais-Royal, METRO: Pyramides
www.yasmine-eslami.com

BESTSELLER
The label's best-selling Serena model pairs transparent organza with a graphic strip of chiffon ribbon (free the nipple!). A permanent fixture for each collection, it's updated in new colors for each season, but always available in a democratic range of sizes, from thirty to thirty-six, and from A to D cups.

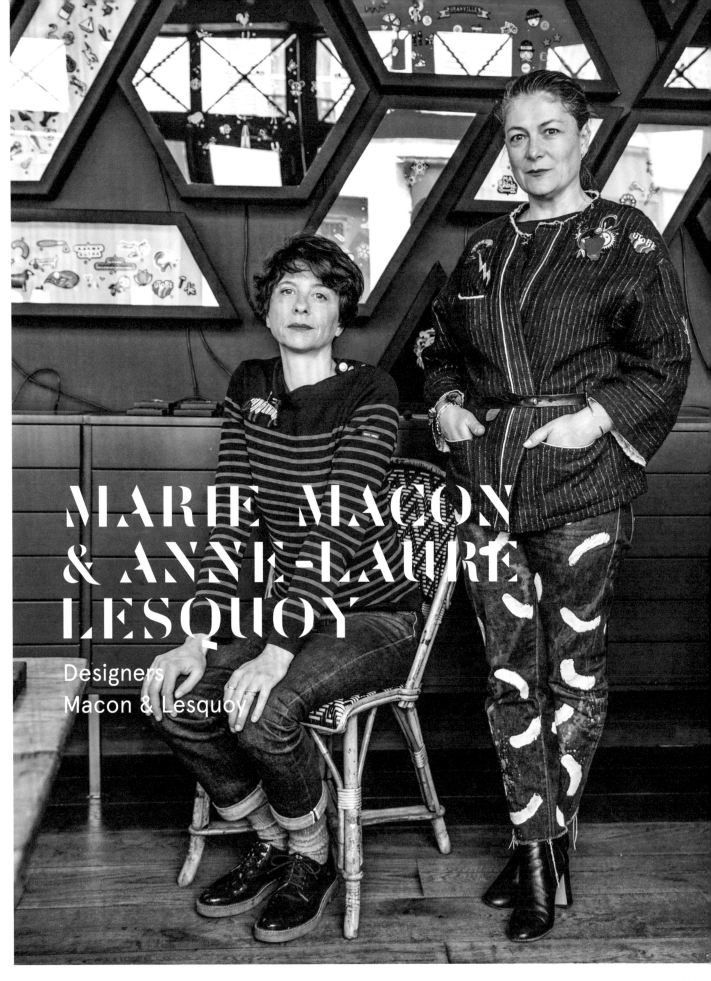

MARIE MACON & ANNE-LAURE LESQUOY

Designers
Macon & Lesquoy

The duo of Macon & Lesquoy design fun and colorful brooches and patches that brighten up any outfit while making a statement about the wearer. A banana, a Camembert, a cigarette, a pigeon, a radish, a sock, an electric guitar.... Like an exquisite set of analog emojis, these beautiful embroidered "jewels" can be combined to create endless visual haikus that cross gender, age, and language barriers for a universal pop appeal.

Marie Macon and Anne-Laure Lesquoy met in 1994 as graduate students at the progressive Paris industrial design school ENSCi. Anne-Laure already had a degree in engineering and product design, Marie in visual communications. "We have two very different approaches," explains Marie. "I look for ideas quite instinctively and quickly, working on mood boards, etc., and Anne-Laure is more focused on fine-tuning the details of the embroidery and the threads. This was already a bit the case when we worked together before."

After graduating, they collaborated regularly for about a decade as freelancers on various projects before stumbling across an extraordinary embroidery atelier in Pakistan, where they were on research for a client. The two friends were instantly smitten with the ancestral technique they discovered there known as goldwork, in which complex motifs are hand embroidered using metallic thread. Originating in Asia, goldwork has existed for millennia and has been used extensively in Europe since the Middle Ages to decorate clothing and furnishings for the church and royalty, and later for military regalia.

When Marie and Anne-Laure didn't manage to convince their client to develop products using this special technique, they decided to take their samples around to a couple of shops in Paris. "We went to see Sarah at Colette and a girl from Merci that I had met at the bakery and they took them right away. They sold really well," explains Marie. Macon & Lesquoy was born. A decade or so later, the two friends sell their much-loved collections worldwide and also from their own funky cabinet of curiosities on the Canal Saint-Martin here in Paris.

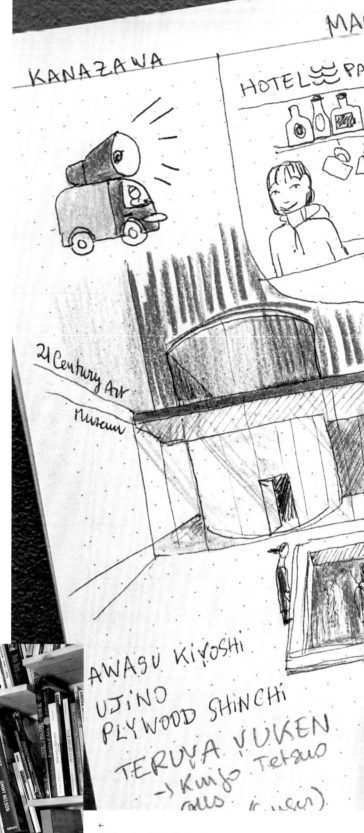

← Shelves loaded with books in the mini studio at the back of the shop—tomes on everything from creating topiary to French fashion designer Thierry Mugler.

TSUNAMI OF LOVE

Petits poèmes
phrases philosophiques,
Citations
Haïku
Brodés & cachés
dans les vêtements
Collection invisible

Tokyo, Detroit. Rwanda. Regular overseas trips provide the inspiration for some of Macon & Lesquoy's two annual collections. "The trip is like a pretext for finding stories to tell. The theme of the collection is usually related to the country we are visiting, but it's not a travel guide. The underlying theme is more political or poetic. When we are traveling, we take notes, Anne-Laure takes photos and I sketch. Then when we return we draw things more precisely. We work the scale, the postures, every detail. Then we do a vector illustration on the computer."

↑
Each Macon & Lesquoy collection includes a flag, that ancient instrument for protest, to defend ideals dear to the house—fraternity, utopia, and liberty are a few recent ones. Here, cotton swatches to help choose the colors.

↓
A tangle of cannetille thread, also known as "French wire" in English. This tube of finely coiled wire is the principal material used by the artisans in Pakistan to create Macon & Lesquoy's precious hand-embroidered brooches.

↓
In addition to the trips abroad, Macon & Lesquoy's creative process is nourished by ongoing collabs with, for example, local pop band The Dø or French actor Romain Duris. Here we see the preparatory drawings for a recent collaboration with the Comédie-Française. The notarial stamp in the bottom right corner protects their designs in case of unlawful copies. "We have a lawyer practically full-time to handle this."

Describe your profession.
We draw, design, sell, do the marketing and PR. We are creators and we run a business. We wear all the hats!

What is unique about your work?
From the beginning we have tried to combine humor with luxury, and it's a very difficult exercise, it doesn't usually go together. Humor is often gimmicky, and quality products are often serious. But we like to laugh; we're pretty stressed-out people, so it's an escape. It makes us laugh to see people wearing anachronistic or offbeat things, or slightly shocking words.

What is luxury?
We make luxury products that are still affordable. We work with embroidery that is entirely done by hand; this is not plastic injection molding! And in addition to being handmade, it's hand-drawn. We draw every one of our designs.

How do you explain your success?
Our products are kind of unclassifiable, neither a brooch nor embroidery, military insignia, or badge. It's not for a man or for a woman. It's something at once funny, extravagant, masculine, that we treat in a really lighthearted way, ultra-modern but at the same time a bit retro. There is a kind of mash-up of codes that is unexpected and that we didn't plan but came about quite naturally.

What do you consider your greatest achievement?
Seeing someone on the subway in Paris or Tokyo wearing one of our creations. That's a great source of pride. And our fanatical customers who collect all our creations, who know what we designed and in what year—that's impressive!

What inspires you?
The relationship with our customers; it's pleasurable, inspiring, rewarding, and it makes us want to keep pushing things forward.

Your favorite tool?
Black Bic pens and color pencils.

↑
Some of the finished pieces from the collab with the Comédie-Française, including a dramatic musketeer-style feathered hat and badges proclaiming "*comedienne!*" or "actress!" Founded in 1680, the once royal theater company is considered the world's oldest active theater company.

Marie Macon & Anne-Laure Lesquoy   219

VISIT

The first and only Macon & Lesquoy boutique opened in 2017 in a former locksmith's atelier close to the Canal Saint-Martin, but also just upwind of Place de la République, where most of Paris's regular public demonstrations start or end. Channeling the spirit of protest and civil liberty of this deeply symbolic civic hub, Macon & Lesquoy named the far wall of their boutique the *mur des revendications* ("protest wall"). Here, every six months, they fly the flag, sometimes quite literally, for their new collection; this season's fresco celebrates "Savanna Night Fever," from their collection inspired by Rwanda.

Macon & Lesquoy
37 rue Yves Toudic,
75010 Paris
Canal Saint-Martin,
METRO: Jacques Bonsergent
www.maconetlesquoy.com

Marie Macon & Anne-Laure Lesquoy

MAXIME BRENON & JULIEN CRESPEL

Stationers
Papier Tigre

"When we started, creatives had completely abandoned stationery in France." Inspired by stuff they discovered on their travels, like the letterpress trend in the US or the brand Moleskine
that was doing basic things really well, Maxime and Julien set up
Paper Tigre in 2012. At first it was a side project to their day job
running Julien's visual communications agency—Julien designing
and Maxime taking care of commercial development. As their
clients transitioned from print to the Web, Julien and Maxime
intuited an opportunity to reconfigure paper's cultural value as
"no longer purely utilitarian," but "something deliberate, beautiful, expressive; a bit like a fashion accessory."

For their first products, they revived snail-mail culture with
bright postcards and fun folded self-mailers, followed by a
range of colorful notebooks that soon became their signature
product. Other bestsellers include a seasonal fruits and vegetables calendar, a graphic memory game, and a weekly desk
planner.

Papier Tigre functioned as an extension to their communications agency, a strategy to inspire their clients with innovative
product design, to usefully fill office downtime, and hopefully
make a few sales on the e-shop. But destiny kicked in in late
2013 when the lease came up on their office. They decided
to move into a shop their friend the designer Matali Crasset
was moving out of in the northern Marais and split the space
between both activities. "One of the most important elements
of our story is to have installed our office inside the shop.
We reduced the distance between the idea and its commerce
to its absolute minimum, and we increased our customers'
proximity to the brand to the maximum."

Papier Tigre's quirky and playful style immediately resonated both locally and abroad, and they soon shut down the
agency to concentrate on developing the company full-time.
Today their boutique is still a hybrid space, but the office has
been replaced by a cutting-edge digital workshop printing out
custom orders for stationery lovers around the world.

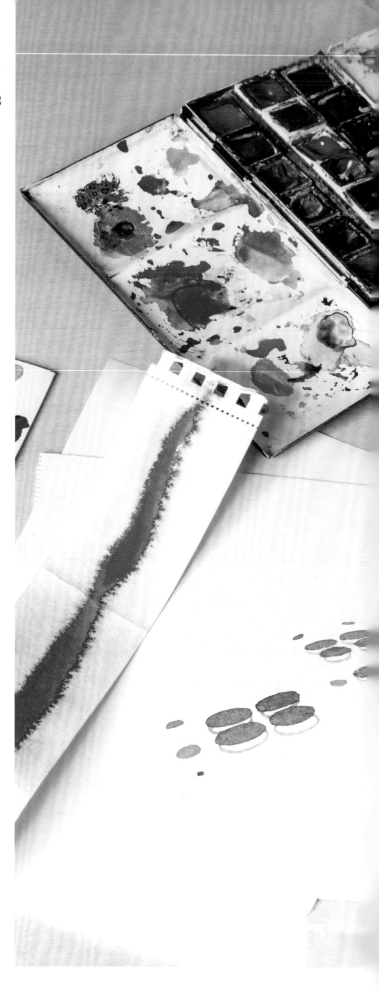

→
"During the creative process, there's no single technique
we use. We do all sorts of tests, photos, drawings, work
on the computer, then we mix it all up. Then maybe we'll
produce a notebook or a planner, or maybe we'll do nothing at all."

Papier Tigre have offered personalization options for their products since the early days. For example, for a small fee you can have up to twenty-six characters in Universe ten-point font stamped in gold on an A5 notebook or the side of a pencil, using a hot foil stamping machine.

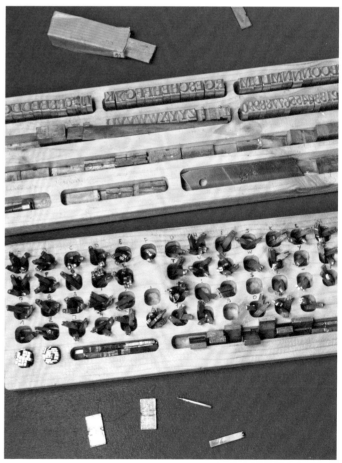

Why do you work where you do?

Historically, this part of Paris was a neighborhood of artisans where there were many workshops. It's always been a neighborhood of people tied to creation, to craft, to design. The 10th, 11th, and 12th arrondissements and the top of the Marais were industrial neighborhoods. So to return with machinery and services here is also to reconnect with the past. It's great to bring that back, to bring craftsmanship back to the center of Paris, which was always a city of people who worked, and not just a tourist city. I think it makes a lot of sense to have both.

Describe your profession.

Initially we were very focused on products but today we are really working between stationery products and services. So that means designing, but also identifying manufacturers, sourcing materials, finding the right prices, finding manufacturing solutions, from time to time even finding machines, finding developers . . . orchestrating all that. And our other job is entrepreneur, which is something that we picked up along the way. Managing teams, people, budgets, schedules, shops, legislation, administration, growth, debt, banks—it's really a whole profession in itself!

What's a typical day for you?

Like everyone, we spend a lot of time answering emails, looking at screens, and having meetings. The rest of the time we try to find the time to think, to create.

What inspires you?

A bit like a fashion brand, every six months we choose a new theme—like Mexico, or space—that allows us to expand our knowledge and our research. It's a ploy to frame our thinking, but it's also reflected in the mood of each collection. We reflect and research visual references. And then we get down to work and produce a fairly large number of propositions. Then in a small group we whittle them down, and then the whole team participates, gives their opinion, and we decide which products will be in the catalog six months later.

How do you explain your success?

We are not afraid to innovate and change things, it's part of our philosophy. If we have an idea, we go for it, we try it out, we see if it works or not. I think that people feel something a little friendly, spontaneous, a bit uninhibited, and this gives the brand strength.

↑
"Increasingly, we are developing accessories around the notebook. That's really what our customers are looking for and it's also what sets us apart from all creative stationery brands. At the moment we are working on small clips to attach your pen to your notebook. We also sell pens, pouches, elastics, and bookmarks."

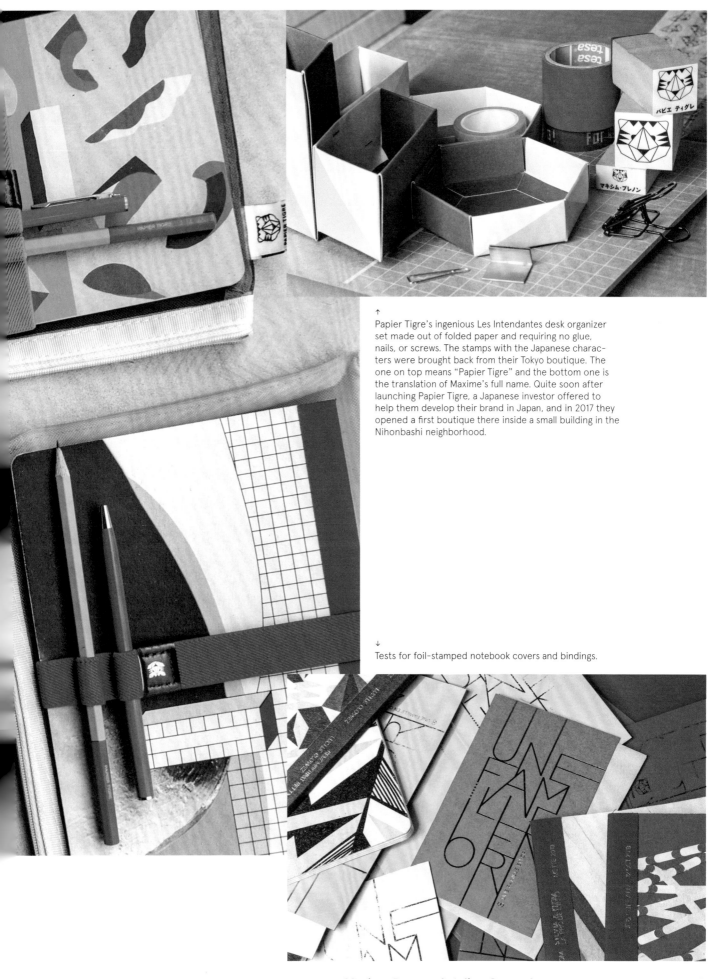

↑

Papier Tigre's ingenious Les Intendantes desk organizer set made out of folded paper and requiring no glue, nails, or screws. The stamps with the Japanese characters were brought back from their Tokyo boutique. The one on top means "Papier Tigre" and the bottom one is the translation of Maxime's full name. Quite soon after launching Papier Tigre, a Japanese investor offered to help them develop their brand in Japan, and in 2017 they opened a first boutique there inside a small building in the Nihonbashi neighborhood.

↓

Tests for foil-stamped notebook covers and bindings.

Maxime Brenon & Julien Crespel

← In 2019 Papier Tigre moved their offices out of the shop to a site around the corner and installed a cutting-edge digital environment comprised of an ecosystem of six or seven different machines for printing, perforation, binding, folding, and trimming. This production site goes hand in hand with a service they launched at the same time allowing clients to design custom notebooks via their website. Options include the notebook's format, paper, cover, binding, orientation, and the organization of the interior pages. "Globalization can go together with the very local. We have managed to set up a local production circuit in Paris and have global exposure and sell around the planet; it goes together. This is the good side of globalization."

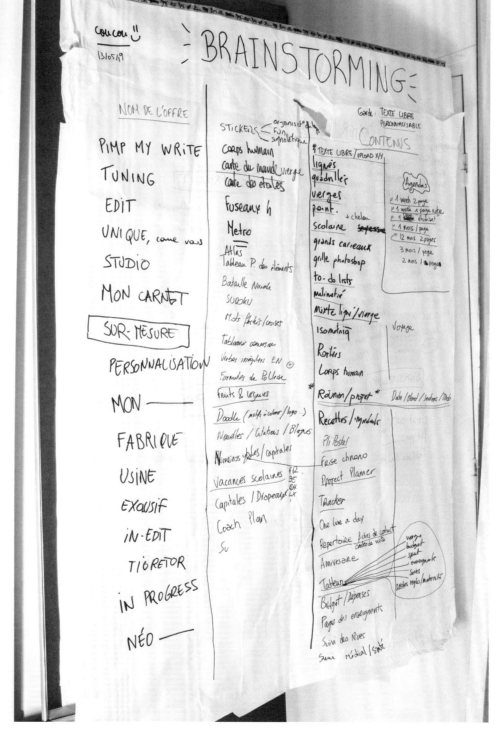

→ The team is always brainstorming new ideas for products, and for innovative new services too.

Maxime Brenon & Julien Crespel

VISIT

Papier Tigre
5 rue des Filles du Calvaire,
75003 Paris
Northern Marais,
METRO: Filles du Calvaire
www.papiertigre.fr

LOGO

"Our name really suits our work and I think our logo has played a role in our success. A 'paper tiger' is originally a Chinese expression describing something that appears very frightening but that is actually very fragile. We inverse it, for us paper is not scary at all, it's fragile, it tears, but if you work on it well, it can become really extraordinary and powerful."

Maxime Brenon & Julien Crespel

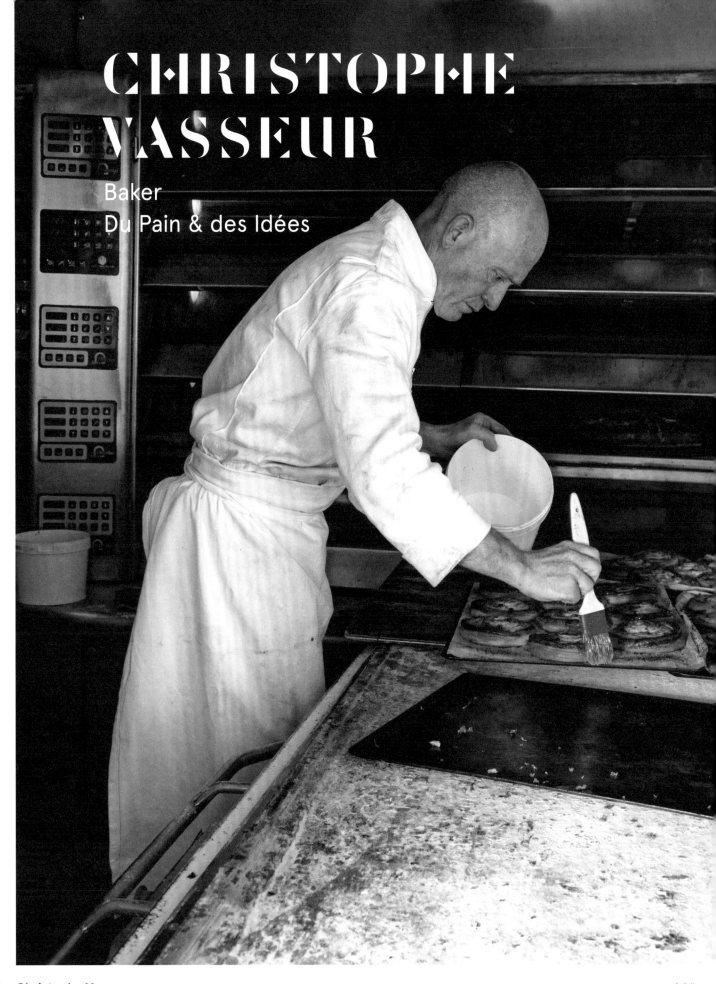

CHRISTOPHE VASSEUR

Baker
Du Pain & des Idées

To step into Christophe Vasseur's bakery is to immerse yourself in a French bakery as it was before the Second World War. You won't find cakes, candy, drinks, or sandwiches, just a short range of breads and *viennoiseries*, or baker's pastries, all made by hand on site. "I didn't invent anything here. My approach was to go back to baking's roots and try to revive traditions that had been forgotten."

A desire to return to something essential had been brewing in Christophe's heart for a couple of years before he took the leap in 2000, at thirty-three years old, quitting his executive job and enrolling in studies to learn the art of baking. Here he discovered that he had an uncommon aptitude, a special intuition, for the breadmaking process, the arts of fermentation and mixing dough, which just confirmed his instincts. If he didn't follow them when he was younger, it was because trades like baker or cook had so little status then, often synonymous with being a high-school dropout.

←
Bakers' couches are used in the preparation of the flutes—Christophe's version of the classic baguette. The loaves are shaped by hand then left to proof in the folds of these linen couches before going in the oven.

←
Throughout the week, Christophe regularly steps out from backstage into the spotlight of his acclaimed bakery, enlivening his beautiful little theater with his passion and personality. "I think personality is very important for a place. Otherwise you may as well be in a chain."

↓
No law in France obliges artisan bakers to prepare their pastries themselves, as they must for their bread. Bakers are free to buy frozen, industrially prepared croissants and simply bake them on site. "The art of making croissants and bakers' pastries hasn't been taught in school for forty years now. When you enter a bakery, eight times out of ten you'll buy an industrial croissant because this knowledge is gone."

Getting his diploma in baking also meant confronting the limitations of the official curriculum that, for example, "taught how to make bread in two hours, not twenty-four." He was obliged to complete his education himself, seeking out old bakers who remembered how things used to be done. Today Christophe is engaged and vocal across the different facets of the craft of baking, from education and training to agricultural practices and legislation. He campaigns against industrial wheat farming and for biodiversity via the cultivation of local and heritage grain varieties.

Three years after leaving his job, Christophe opened his bakery Du Pain & des Idées behind the Canal Saint-Martin. The heritage site has operated as a bakery for 150 years and conserves many original features like the beautiful painted ceiling and the beveled mirrors. Monday to Friday, a stream of customers come here to enjoy Christophe's exceptional bread and pastries, all the result of uncompromising attention and care. "What I wanted and still want is to give happiness to people with something made with my hands, but putting my heart, guts, and brain into it too." The tables out front invite pilgrims to sit and break bread together, feeding their body and their spirit.

Christophe Vasseur

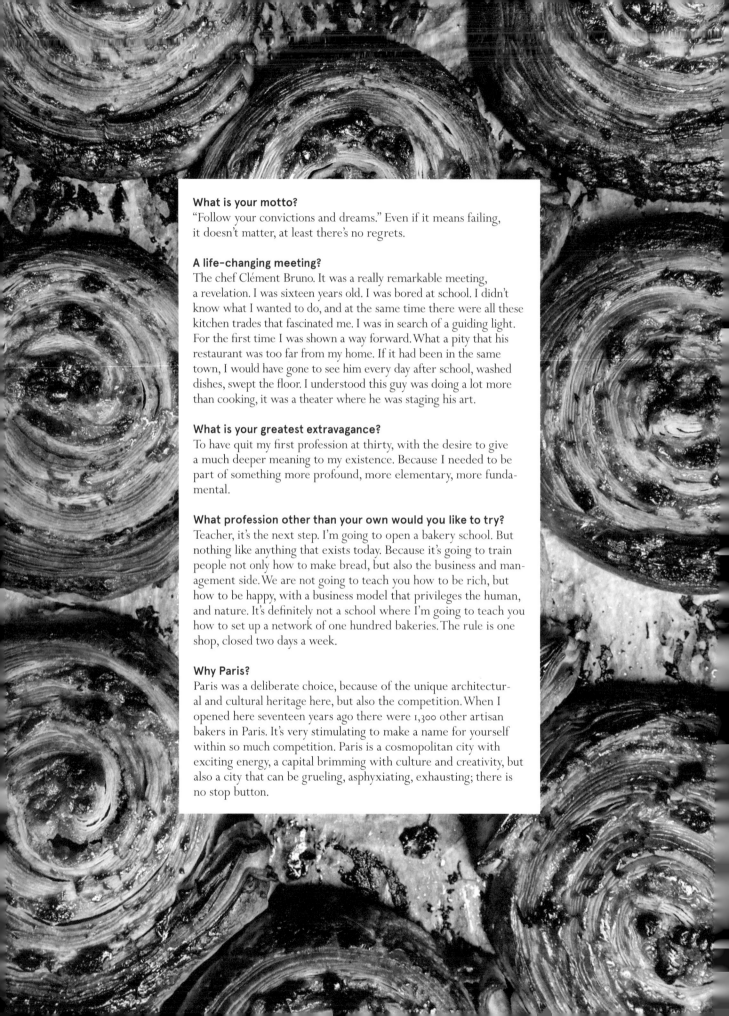

What is your motto?

"Follow your convictions and dreams." Even if it means failing, it doesn't matter, at least there's no regrets.

A life-changing meeting?

The chef Clément Bruno. It was a really remarkable meeting, a revelation. I was sixteen years old. I was bored at school. I didn't know what I wanted to do, and at the same time there were all these kitchen trades that fascinated me. I was in search of a guiding light. For the first time I was shown a way forward. What a pity that his restaurant was too far from my home. If it had been in the same town, I would have gone to see him every day after school, washed dishes, swept the floor. I understood this guy was doing a lot more than cooking, it was a theater where he was staging his art.

What is your greatest extravagance?

To have quit my first profession at thirty, with the desire to give a much deeper meaning to my existence. Because I needed to be part of something more profound, more elementary, more fundamental.

What profession other than your own would you like to try?

Teacher, it's the next step. I'm going to open a bakery school. But nothing like anything that exists today. Because it's going to train people not only how to make bread, but also the business and management side. We are not going to teach you how to be rich, but how to be happy, with a business model that privileges the human, and nature. It's definitely not a school where I'm going to teach you how to set up a network of one hundred bakeries. The rule is one shop, closed two days a week.

Why Paris?

Paris was a deliberate choice, because of the unique architectural and cultural heritage here, but also the competition. When I opened here seventeen years ago there were 1,300 other artisan bakers in Paris. It's very stimulating to make a name for yourself within so much competition. Paris is a cosmopolitan city with exciting energy, a capital brimming with culture and creativity, but also a city that can be grueling, asphyxiating, exhausting; there is no stop button.

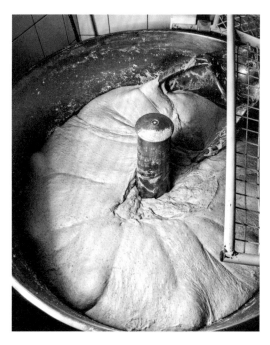

←
"I mix the dough very little, just five minutes on the first speed, twenty minutes in second, and five minutes in third speed. It's as if I have kneaded it by hand."

←
At Du Pain et des Idées, *escargot* pastries—a standard in French bakeries—come not only with the usual sultana filling, but in four or five flavors that Christophe has created. He might add to the house-made pastry cream: rum-infused Smyrna sultanas; hazelnuts, lemon, and honey; almond praline; berries and cream cheese; fresh blackcurrants and kirsch; or chocolate chip and pistachio. "The chocolate-pistachio has become world famous, people post selfies with it all around Paris, it's a real phenomenon!"

↓
Niflettes, a regional specialty from Provins, are made with croissant dough and pastry cream and traditionally eaten on All Saints' Day. Christophe presents a number of recipes in his bakery that are largely unknown outside their regions, like the *sacristain*, a crunchy twist of croissant pastry with pastry cream native to the city of Montélimar; the recipe for his Mouna brioche, perfumed with orange flower water, originates from North Africa.

↑
A dough cutter and scraper. "Dough is like a muscle; you mustn't tear it or pull on it, you have to cut it."

Christophe Vasseur

VISIT

SPECIALTY

Christophe's signature bread is the Pain des Amis ("bread of friends"), invoking one of bread's elemental functions: bringing people together. It also "embodies exactly what craftsmanship should be, that is to say a man or a woman who transforms raw materials to make a unique and singular work." The bread is made with yeast, not sourdough, which allows the flavors of the wheat to fully express themselves. The dough is fermented slowly for two days, hand-shaped, then baked for an hour on stone, which explains its deep golden crust, sweet and smokey fragrance, and flat bottom.

Du Pain & des Idées
34 rue Yves Toudic,
75010 Paris
Canal Saint Martin,
METRO: Jacques Bonsergent
www.dupainetdesidees.com

PAIN DES AMIS
Un pain tout en croûte,
légèrement fumé.
Farine biologique.

250g / 500g
2,85€ / 5,7€

Christophe Vasseur —

PIERRE COULON

Cheesemaker
La Laiterie de Paris

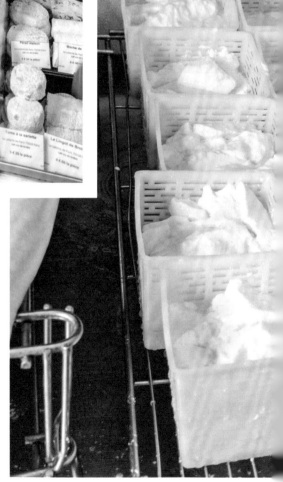

At the Laiterie you can pick up a bottle of small producer wine to go with your cheese or bring your own bottle and fill it from the cask of organic wine. A truly neighborhood shop, Laiterie also sells a number of fermented milk products traditionally consumed in Muslim countries, such as leben, kefir, labneh, or rayeb, to the many local North African immigrants.

In 2017, Pierre Coulon opened an urban cheese shop the likes of which Paris had never seen. Yes, La Laiterie de Paris sells a range of French and foreign cheeses that are matured on site, but what makes La Laiterie unique is that they make their own cheese as well. "Make cheese great again!" goes their slogan.

Great cheese starts with great milk. The Laiterie buys raw, organic sheep, goat, and cow milk direct from producers in Normandy and Brittany to make their own recipes or versions of traditional recipes, like French Brillat-Savarin, Saint-Félicien, or Saint-Marcellin, Cypriot halloumi, and English cheddar. If the Laiterie pays their milk producers double or triple the market rate, it has very strict requirements, working with, for example, only grass-fed animals. "Quality starts at the source; it starts with the happiness of the animal; it starts with the size of the farm. We prefer small farms, and we also want to work with people who are implicated in their land, that grow their own feed, whose farm corresponds to the size of the herd."

Upon completing a degree in agronomy with a focus on goats and cheese, Pierre ran a dairy farm of 140 goats and sixty ewes just north of his native Nantes. Five years later, in 2014, he returned to city life and took up a position as assistant director for the prestigious Parisian cheesemonger Androuet. Then in 2015, as part of a lifelong quest to complete his education, Pierre quit his job and hit the road with a backpack and a map of the forty-five or so *Appellation d'origine protégée* (AOP) cheeses of France. He turned up at farms, offering to work in exchange for instruction on cheesemaking. Originally planned for six months, the journey turned into a two-year epic not just in France, but throughout Europe, Canada, and even America. His blog documenting the journey went viral, laying the foundations for what would become La Laiterie de Paris.

Inspired by all the passionate people he met, the extraordinary cheeses he tasted, and the innovative urban cheesemaking ventures he came across in cities like London and New York, Pierre decided to synthesize his vast knowledge into his own venture. In February 2017 he launched a crowdfunding campaign, and in December La Laiterie de Paris opened its doors. Here in the heart of Paris's popular Goutte d'Or neighborhood, Pierre and the rest of the Laiterie team go back to the future, reviving the traditional art of cheesemaking while connecting their urban cheese-loving clients to France's farmers, herds, and pastures.

↑
The cheeses are left to ripen and age in a cellar in which the humidity and temperature are carefully controlled. This is the final step in the cheesemaking process, when the living organisms inside and outside the cheese are allowed to develop more fully, enriching the flavor, texture, and aroma. These cheeses will ripen for a few weeks, while other varieties of hard cheese produced at Laiterie, like Charolais or Tomme, can be aged longer, up to four or six months. The pink clothespins are marked with the date the cheeses entered the cellar. On the top tray is Lyca, Laiterie's version of Saint-Marcellin, a cow's milk cheese; underneath, sheep's milk lingots. On the third tray, the sheep's milk Tome à la Sarriette, which will be coated with the herb savory after ripening. And on the bottom shelf, the goat's cheese Labat, a *cendré* variety, is coated with ash.

←
Goat curds drain in molds. The curds on the right are yellow from being infused with organic French saffron grown in Normandy. After two or three weeks of ripening, the Tomme-style cheese will be available to buy in the shop.

↑
Pierre and his team are constantly experimenting with new recipes, inspired by ingredients and techniques discovered on their travels. "We really pay attention to the quality of our spices and other condiments. We always make sure these raw materials are visible in the shop for our customers to see; we are proud to display our beautiful sugar, our beautiful pepper...."

Describe your work.
We make cheese in Paris. Surprisingly, nobody had ever done this before us. Half of what we sell is made by us here and the rest are cheeses selected by us and aged here. I don't select products if I have not personally met the producer, at least once, but many of the producers are friends.

What is unique about your work?
We wanted to return to the most basic traditions. When we make cheese, it's just milk, ferments, rennet, and salt—basta! We really wanted to perpetuate this farmhouse simplicity, to continue with very simple things.

Your favorite tool?
The cheesemaker's ladle. We also use saucepans, whisks, molds, a copper cauldron too … it's really a simple profession; there are no machines.

What inspires you?
My travels. For example, I was in London and I saw that everyone was eating halloumi. But what you find today is very industrial, very salty; a far cry from what was done in the past. So we went and found the original recipe.

What is unique about Paris?
It's a city with lots of energy, which feeds my own vitality. And for me Paris is where you find the most energy around food in the world. There's a huge number of local specialty shops here. There's really an *art de vivre* in this city that is very cool.

Gouda de chèvre Bio

Treur Woarden Pays Bas
Lait pasteurisé de chèvre

44 € 50 le kilo

↑
As well as their own production, Laiterie sells many cheeses Pierre has
selected from different producers
that he has met throughout France,
but also further afield in Europe and
England, like this organic goat's milk
Gouda from Holland.

Le Labat

La Laiterie de Paris 75018 Paris

Lait cru de chèvre

6 € 00 la pièce

Myrha
affiné à la bière de la Brasserie de la Goutte d'Or
La Laiterie de Paris 75018 Paris
Lait cru de vache

33 € 50 le kilo

20% MG

←
Flying the flag for the local neighborhood, a number of the Laiterie's
cheeses are named after streets in
the Goutte d'Or. For example the
Myrha, flavored with beer from local
craft brewery the Brasserie de la
Goutte d'Or; the Labat; or the Pavé
des Poissonniers.

VISIT

La Laiterie de Paris
74 rue des Poissonniers, 75018 Paris
La Goutte d'Or, METRO: Marcadet-Poissonniers
Instagram: @laiterie_de_paris_fromagerie_

BEYOND CHEESE

As well as cheese, Laiterie sells other milk-based products, always prepared with the finest raw materials to uphold their dedication to quality and flavor. The seasonal selection of yogurts might include hazelnut, prepared with nuts from Piedmont infused in hot milk prior to fermentation, or strawberry, perfumed with a housemade jam made from organic, French, soil-grown berries and sugar. A rice pudding might come perfumed with matcha, black sesame, or vanilla. Or just buy the great organic milk and make your own at home.

Pierre Coulon –

JACQUES GENIN

Chocolatier, confectioner, pâtissier
Jacques Genin

Like a fairy tale, Jacques Genin's life contains magic and tragic darkness, where poverty and violence are transformed into sweet, melting mouthfuls of chocolate, nougat, caramel, or marshmallow. Fleeing a violent home in Saint-Dié-des-Vosges in northeastern France, Jacques left school at just twelve years old to start an apprenticeship in a local abattoir. His boss was harsh but fair, and took the young Jacques under his wing; when this mentor died, Jacques packed up and hitched a ride to the capital.

Arriving in Paris at nineteen years old, he soon picked up work in a restaurant—that "last refuge of the misfit ... a place for people with bad pasts to find a new family," to quote Anthony Bourdain. Saint-Germain-des-Prés in the 1980s was a hub of hedonism and culture, a whirlwind of fine food, jazz, night life, and literature exposing Jacques to an abundance of new worlds. And with Jacques's capacity for hard work, his drive and ambition soon took him from waiting tables to cooking in his own restaurant, learning as he went along, always hungry for knowledge.

Then in 1990, on his reputation as a master of precision and flavor, the gourmet chocolate chain La Maison du Chocolat invited Genin to develop its pâtisserie line. He spent six years perfecting their chocolate tart and éclair before striking out on his own, setting up a specialist food lab where for over a decade he and his team produced exquisite chocolates and confectionaries for some of the city's best chefs and restaurants.

In a bold new move, Jacques Genin came out of the shadows in 2009 to open an airy, two-story boutique in the northern Marais where he sells the delicious chocolates for which he is famous, but also all sorts of other sweet delights like caramel, ice cream, and classic French pâtisserie. Everything is prepared upstairs in the lab, where Jacques and his team work with only the best fresh produce. In this story, happiness triumphs, culture heals, and hard work and ambition provide sweet emancipation.

↑
The day's cake orders on the note board. Jacques Genin cakes are one of Paris's best kept secrets, only available for takeaway orders. Depending on the season, choose from a short menu that might feature his famous lime and basil tart, mille-feuille, custard, strawberry, raspberry, and chocolate tarts, and cheesecake.

←
A new batch of chocolates pass through the enrobing machine. "A balance between sour, bitterness, sweet; between crunch, creaminess; it's an ensemble of things, and above all it's a fresh product." Jacques Genin chocolates might come flavored with chestnut honey, Tonka bean, Sichuan pepper, ginger, raspberry, grapefruit, bergamot, mint, basil, capers, and more. Containing no preservatives, the chocolates must be eaten within ten days.

→
A batch of caramel on the stove.

Pâtisserie is starting to get a bad rap as the last gastronomic domain that doesn't fly the flag of the seasonal, local, and organic. Jacques, however, uses zero frozen or industrial ingredients. He prefers fresh butter, milk, and cream; sugar over glucose syrup; cocoa butter over hydrogenated fats; and fresh fruit over frozen purées. He rejects artificial coloring, texturants, thickeners, emulsifiers, flavors, and preservatives. His attention to the raw materials and flavor is second nature after decades working as a chef.

A seasonal recipe only available for the few summer months when the berries are in season, Jacques's strawberry tart piles juicy, field-grown strawberries on top of a frangipane almond cream inside a crispy pastry shell. A few raspberries hide inside for a touch of acidity. "My cakes are really well garnished. I sell dreams, so if it's not generous, something's wrong."

Jacques Genin

→
Genin only uses fresh whole eggs in his recipes; many *pâtissiers* use industrial, pasteurized egg mixes.

↑
Incredible taste bombs, Jacques's fruit jellies are concentrations of flavor direct from the garden or orchard depending on the season and Jacques's inspiration—perhaps lychee, fennel, beetroot, rhubarb, cucumber, or pear.

Why Paris?
Paris made me what I am today simply through meeting people. I tell myself that from where I come from, I've been lucky to meet so many people in my life, to rub shoulders with the great and the good.

What is your favorite neighborhood in Paris?
I knew the last days of Les Halles. I had nothing then, so if there was a truck to unload, I unloaded the truck. The guy paid you right away, he brought you a meal. I went to really amazing bars in the morning, where you met all kinds of people. It was just fabulous. And I knew Saint-Germain in the 1980s. The Saint-Germain I know today is nothing like it used to be.

Your most delightful encounter?
I was working in a restaurant in Paris and I met a man called Joël Roret, a figure in local government. He was a regular and one day he left a bag behind. I don't know why I didn't give him back his bag, but I kept it and I took it home. There were books inside: *Demian*, *Der Steppenwolf*, *Siddhartha*, and *Narcissus and Goldmund* by Herman Hesse; *Confusion* by Stefan Zweig; *The Abyss* by Marguerite Yourcenar. I started with *Demian*, and I didn't understand a thing. I was nineteen years old. I decided to buy a Larousse dictionary to decipher the words. At the start it was very, very hard. But I started to become fully conscious when I began to read.

How do you explain your success?
I think that I always had a certain curiosity inside me. When I was a kid, I was a dreamer, but I quickly understood that where I came from, they wanted to break my dreams. Until the age of thirty, I hated the adult world. Except at a certain point, I had this curiosity, to meet other people, to know another world, to perhaps create my own world.

Your favorite tool?
My finest tool is the human being. Above all, I need human relationships. The rest, the equipment, is not important.

What is unique about your work?
The work of a craftsman is repetition. Are you able to do everything exactly the same from January 1 to December 31? It's hard.

Describe your profession.
My job is to try to be happy.

↑
To flavor his delicious walnut and honey caramel tartlet, Genin uses only quality Périgord walnuts and chestnut honey.

←
Chocolate truffles. Rich and velvety concentrations of chocolate flavor combining cream, butter, and chocolate and dusted with bitter cocoa.

VISIT

Jacques Genin
133 rue de Turenne, 75003 Paris
Northern Marais,
METRO: République or Filles du Calvaire
www.jacquesgenin.fr

SPECIALTY

A pleasure to say and especially to eat, the Paris-Brest is one of the classics of French pâtisserie. A baked choux pastry round is filled with a rich praline buttercream making for a unique combination of creaminess, airiness, nuttiness, and crunch. The story goes that the cake was invented in 1910 by Louis Durand, a pâtissier from the Paris region, in the shape of a bicycle wheel to commemorate the round-trip cycling race between Paris and Brest. Jacques's lofty version of the classic cake has a few extra centimeters of filling, and is scattered with roasted hazelnuts rather than the usual slithered almonds. Each cake is prepared to order using fine ingredients and never sees the inside of a refrigerator.

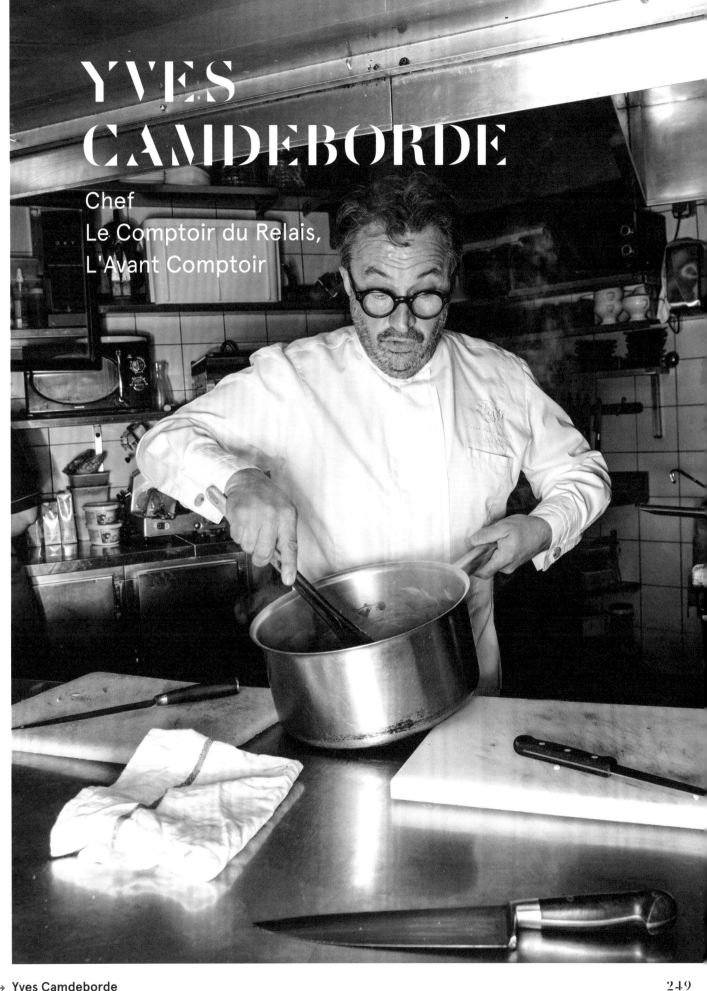

YVES CAMDEBORDE

Chef
Le Comptoir du Relais,
L'Avant Comptoir

Today, Paris is home to an array of relaxed and affordable restaurants run by talented, creative chefs, but in the 1980s, good restaurants were typically expensive and stuffy. Chef Yves Camdeborde is credited with pioneering the "bistronomy" movement in Paris in the early 1990s, marrying the relaxed atmosphere and prices of a local bistro with the ambition and technique of French *haute gastronomie*.

After more than a decade working in the kitchen brigades of some of the most prestigious restaurants in Paris, including the Ritz, the Crillon, and La Tour d'Argent, at just twenty-eight years old Camdeborde struck out on his own and opened his own place. "The grand restaurants are magical, but I was at the theater where I had a role to play, I had my score, but I was never myself. I knew that I was going to be spending the rest of my life working in a restaurant, so it was my goal to stop playing a role and just be me."

For over a decade, at the much-loved La Régalade, Yves served up refined dishes like squid-ink risotto or Grand Marnier soufflé on a set thirty-euro, three-course menu. He worked with expensive produce like lobster, but also equally flavorsome ingredients that were usually ignored in fine dining restaurants, such as beef cheek, pig's trotters, mackerel, or sardines. The dining room and service were unpretentious and usually boisterous—a revolution. Then in 2004, Camdeborde, who was ready for a new challenge, sold to his second in command. Today he's at the head of a small empire at the heart of Saint-Germain-des-Prés, comprising a boutique hotel, his restaurant le Comptoir du Relais, and a constellation of gourmet neighborhood wine bars called l'Avant-Comptoir.

The recipe remains the same at each establishment—good food and good vibes centered around great produce. His website proudly lists his favorite suppliers, with a particular attention to produce from his native Béarn region, including *andouillette* and black sausage from his family's charcuterie business in Pau, but also butter and eggs from Normandy, oysters from Brittany, honey from Corsica, black truffles and organic veggies from Provence, wines from Burgundy ... all faithful partners from the four corners of France who provide the raw materials for Camdeborde to express French terroir and tradition, but especially to satisfy his quest for personal expression and sincerity.

←
"When I arrived in Paris, the chef at the Ritz, Guy Legay talked to me about 'good produce,' which I had never heard of. He explained that it's a carrot or a strawberry that is grown in soil, or a calf that has only known its mother's milk. I'm from the country, this is normal. What's happening today, with locavore, with natural wines, etc., is we're obliged to put superlatives on normality."

POÊLÉE DU JOUR
CABILLAUD
CAROTTES, BROCOLIS,
POIS GOURMANDS
PETIS POIS, COURGETTE,
RADIS ROSES,
FLEUR, HERBES,
UNE RÂGATE

↑
Hunks of great sourdough to mop up
the sauces and juices made by his
friend, the chef Thierry Breton, who
delivers it himself each morning on
his bike. Slathered with some of the
salted Bordier butter on the counter,
it's a meal in itself.

→
On the menu at the Avant Comptoir
de la Mer, pan-fried *chipirons*,
or calamari, from Saint-Jean-de-Luz,
the main coastal town of Yves's native
Béarn region in Southwest France.
It was a popular dish at La Régalade
back in the 1990s.

What do you consider your greatest achievement?

We made fine cooking accessible to all. We threw away the rule book. We said we'll do what we want. We're free. After the Ritz, the Crillon, I wanted to put the same quality on the plate, the same gastronomic consideration, but change the attitudes and comportment. For me, coming from the south, from farmer parents, a restaurant should be a place of conviviality. A place where you're allowed to laugh, you're allowed to turn up in a pair of shorts, where there is life!

What is your greatest extravagance?

I love to eat. My passion is restaurants, I go to restaurants all the time. I'm an insatiable eater. Really a very, very big eater. I have to be really careful, otherwise I put on weight. It's not easy.

What is unique about your activity?

French cuisine is made in the saucepan, in the frying pan, not on the plate. It's not assembly cooking, it's cooking with complexity. Today, globalized cuisine—which is also interesting—happens on the plate. Which is to say you bring ingredients, exceptional ingredients, and arrange them on a plate. French cuisine takes place on the stove, seasoning, deglazing, sautéing. This is the French gastronomic tradition.

What is unique about Paris?

It was magical coming to Paris because everything is possible here. It's very progressive and broad minded. Here people aren't judged on appearances but rather on depth. If someone is different from us we look at them, we listen to them. I come from the country, and there, you don't listen to foreigners. Even today in regional France, as soon as you are a foreigner, even from a different region—a guy from the Southeast who goes to the Southwest—you're looked at strangely. Whereas in Paris we just look at people like human beings.

What is your favorite neighborhood in Paris?

I live by the Place d'Aligre, I love it there because it is such a mix of different cultures and classes: French, North African, working class, wealthy…. And when you're at the market you talk to everyone, there's a very open-minded spirit. It's very enriching.

A life-changing meeting?

The first, the most essential, the most vital meeting was with Christian Constant. He was second in command to Guy Legay at the Ritz when I arrived in Paris. He took me under his wing. He saw a young guy show up from the Southwest, a bit wet behind the ears, and he protected me from all the Parisian bullshit. And he also really brought out team spirit in me. That was his greatest strength. In 1988 he built an incredible team at the Crillon. Jean-François Piège, Emmanuel Renaut, Thierry Breton, Thierry Faucher … we spent three, four years together and lived something very intense thanks to Mr. Constant. We worked like crazy, but with this human cohesion and mutual respect of each other. He looked past our faults; he knew that I was always complaining, that Jean-François gets in a huff, but it's not important, everyone's different. That's the spirit that he passed on to me.

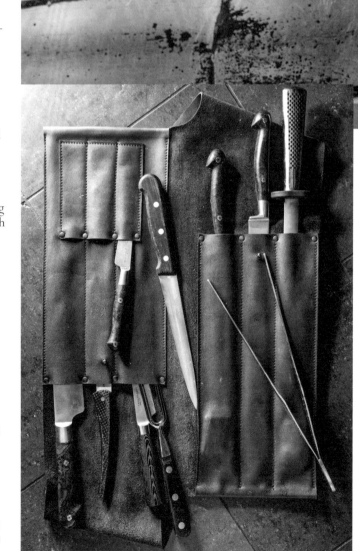

←
Ever since he opened La Régalade in 1992, Yves has been a champion of natural wines by trailblazing winemakers such as Marcel Lapierre, Pierre Overnoy, Dard & Ribo, Françoise Dutheil de la Rochère, and the Amoreau family. "I had the chance to meet Marcel Lapierre, a natural-wine pioneer in France, who is deceased today. He came to see me, he tasted my cooking, and he said to me, 'Yves, we do the same thing.' He brought me a lot in relation to my thinking about wine."

→
The unsheathed knife with the wooden handle was Yves's very first knife, acquired when he began his chef's apprenticeship at age 14. "Knives are a cook's companion. Every day we sharpen our knives and every day before going home we thank them. The right knife makes all the difference when you fillet a fish, carve meat, chop some parsley or carrots. If your knife has a good blade and you cut in the right direction, you get a beautiful neat slice and you don't crush the raw material. It's important to keep the juices in."

VISIT

Le Comptoir du Relais
9 Carrefour de l'Odéon, 75006 Paris
Saint-Germain-des-Prés, METRO: Odéon
www.camdeborde.com

L'Avant Comptoir de la Terre
L'Avant Comptoir de la Mer
3 Carrefour de l'Odéon, 75006 Paris
Saint-Germain-des-Prés, METRO: Odéon
www.camdeborde.com

L'Avant Comptoir du Marché
14 rue Lobineau, 75006 Paris
Saint-Germain-des-Prés,
METRO: Odéon or Mabillon
www.camdeborde.com

A NEIGHBORHOOD EMPIRE

Camdeborde's flagship restaurant Le Comptoir du Relais is installed on the ground floor of his hotel Le Relais Saint Germain. At lunchtime and on the weekends, it's open without reservation all afternoon from noon, serving a generous menu of French brasserie classics. In the evenings, the tables are dressed with white linen, and Yves proposes a sixty-euro tasting menu that explores more sophisticated recipes and produce; it's booked up about a month in advance. In 2009, Yves took over an empty site next door and opened Avant Comptoir de la Terre, a modern wine and tapas bar serving lots of delicious, seasonal small plates. In 2016, he opened another one, a little further down the street, with a seafood focus, Avant Comptoir de la Mer. A third soon followed inside the nearby Saint Germain covered market. Open nonstop from noon to midnight, his three and counting Avant Comptoirs are exquisitely informal spots to drop in for a hit of popular French dining culture squished up at the zinc bar.

Yves Camdeborde

Acknowledgments

What a privilege to make this book, to meet these makers.
They've deepened our understanding of life in Paris, indeed of life.
Thank you.

Thank you Patti Smith for your blessing and your example.

The idea for this book sprung forth practically fully formed
the day Carrie looked over her shoulder—we were sharing
a workspace in Paris—and hit me with, "My editor has asked
me to throw some ideas his way." It's been a long and winding
road since then. Thanks to Sarah Smith from David Black Agency
for her enthusiasm. Our editor Holly La Due and the entire team
at Prestel (with a special mention to Anjali Pala and Ayesha
Wadhawan) are expert at making great books. We could never
make up our minds whether our friends José Albergaria and
Rik Bas Backer of Change is Good should be in the book or
design it. Thanks to Aubane Favier and the team at the Fondation
Cartier for their assistance; what pros! A shout-out to our intern,
Winston Papadopoulos.

And on a more personal note, thanks to my improvised,
international editorial committee: Nadine Davidoff, Linda
Fallon, Clodagh Kinsella, Alexandra Marshall, Sophie Peyrard,
Jayne Tuttle, and Melissa Unger. Other friends for their goodwill
and unerring enthusiasm: Isabelle Ballu, Ludivine Billaud,
Jemma Birrell, Louise Blackwell, Zahava Elenberg, Vallejo Gantner,
Emilie Meinadier, Nina Safaina, Anna Watts, and Amy Wood-Walter.
When I was lacking inspiration, Sally Ross's painting *Garçons*
provided some. To Jill Bartlett for helping establish the perfect
Burgundy writer's retreat. To Anna and Morry Schwartz,
thanks again.

A few songs that helped set the mood while I typed: Patti Smith's
"People Have the Power," Suicide's "Dream Baby Dream,"
The Modern Lovers' "Pablo Picasso," Amy Winehouse's
"Some Unholy War," Leonard Cohen's "Who By Fire," PJ Harvey's
"Horses in My Dreams," Gillian Welch's "Elvis Presley Blues,"
The Velvet Underground's "I'm Set Free," Nick Cave & The
Bad Seeds' "Push the Sky Away," Bob Dylan's "A Hard Rain's
a-Gonna Fall," Cat Power's "The Greatest," and Bill Callahan's
"One Fine Morning."

Extra special thanks to my fellow travellers Gilles and
Lee Tombeur. And to my brother Jason, the first maker I knew.

—

Follow Makers online and on Instagram
mkrs.family #mkrsfamily #mkrsparis